Fine WoodWorking

design
book
seven

Fine WoodWorking

design book seven

360 photographs of the best work in wood

The Taunton Press

Front-cover photographs (clockwise from top):
GEOFFREY NODEN
Trenton, N.J.
Arched-top chair
(see p. 30)
Photo by Michael Slack

LARRY HAAS
Portsmouth, N.H.
Dresser
(see p. 129)
Photo by Karosis Photographic

HENRY R. LINDER, JR.
Roseville, Minn.
Drinks cabinet
(see p. 22)
Photo by Chris Schafer

JOHN T. SHARP
Kent, Ohio
"Still Life with Mallard & Apples"
(see p. 135)
Photo by Gary Miller

ROBERT DIEMERT
Dundas, Ont., Canada
End table
(see p. 58)
Photo by Jeremy Jones

DEWEY GARRETT
Livermore, Calif.
"Analysis #2"
(see p. 151)
Photo by Jim Ferreira

Back-cover photographs:
Top: *JANICE C. SMITH*
Lawrence, Kans.
"Lateen"
(see p. 34)
Photo by Reuben P. Wade

Bottom left: *DALE BROHOLM*
Wellesley, Mass.
Four-sided tall case clock
(see p. 171)
Photo by Dean Powell

Bottom center: *STEVEN ANDERSEN*
Seattle, Wash.
"Oval Hole Arched-Top Guitar"
(see p. 170)
Photo by Stacey Schofield

Bottom right: *LANCE PATTERSON*
Boston, Mass.
Queen Anne highboy
(see p. 89)
Photo by Lance Patterson

Taunton
BOOKS & VIDEOS
for fellow enthusiasts

©1996 by The Taunton Press
All rights reserved.

First printing: 1996
Printed in the United States of America

A FINE WOODWORKING book

FINE WOODWORKING® is a trademark of The Taunton Press, Inc.
registered in the U.S. Patent and Trademark Office.

The Taunton Press, 63 South Main Street, Box 5506,
Newtown, CT 06470-5506

Library of Congress Cataloging-in-Publication Data

Design book seven : 360 photographs of the best work in wood.
        p.   cm.
     At head of title: Fine woodworking
     ISBN 1-56158-124-0
        1. Furniture design—History—20th century—Catalogs.
     2. Furniture—Styles—Catalogs.   I. Fine woodworking.
     NK2395.D47   1996
     749.2'049'075—dc20   96-8879
                                                  CIP

contents

introduction

Nearly two decades have passed since we published our first *Design Book*. In those years, we've seen many changes in both the publishing and woodworking fields. In publishing, there's been tremendous growth. When we produced the first issue of *Fine Woodworking* in 1975, it was the only woodworking magazine available. There are currently more than a dozen magazines on the market. Now more than ever, the woodworking enthusiast has access to a broad source of information on project plans, ideas, tips and techniques.

This dramatic increase is just one indication of the escalating interest in woodworking. Current surveys indicate there are more than 20 million people involved in some form of woodworking. It's no surprise that an entire mail-order industry has evolved to provide these woodworkers with instant access to virtually any tool, hardware item or species of wood—no matter where they live.

Accelerated growth like this is often the impetus to change. Whether in publishing or woodworking, it forces you to focus on what you're doing, to refine your work, to make it the best it can be. These changes and refinements are evident if you've followed our publications over the years. The first 47 issues of *Fine Woodworking* and the first three *Design Books* were black and white. Undeniably this gives them a classic look, but there's nothing quite like seeing a fine piece of furniture in color (except of course, seeing it in person). So with the advent of more powerful, faster computers and the proliferation of new printing technologies, we gladly embraced these improvements and made the exciting change to color.

Although the changes in *Design Book Seven* aren't as noticeable as switching from black and white to color, they're just as important. For example, we've greatly increased the number of detail shots to give you a close-up look at exemplary details: an inlaid design, a handmade pull or a set of exquisite dovetails on a desk drawer. We've also added a new graphic to help tie the information about the maker and the piece to the photograph.

You also may notice a shift in the furniture styles selected for this book. As in the past, the pieces shown here are representative of the best current work in wood. But the majority of the submitted work (more than 2,300 pieces) were practical in design, superbly executed and highly refined. There was also a surprising number of interpretations of traditional styles: delightful pieces that showed a distinct mission, flavor or perhaps a touch of Art Deco. What we didn't receive were large numbers of studio or art furniture. Some of this is surely the result of the influence of well-known craftsmen and teachers like James Krenov, Wendell Castle, Tage Frid, Sam Maloof and Jere Osgood. It may also be the result of refinements and changes in tastes of woodworkers and their patrons alike.

I'd like to thank everyone who submitted entries and encourage you to do the same for our next *Design Book*. And finally, I'd like to express my appreciation to all those who took time out of their busy work schedules to help out with the judging: Scott Gibson, Tim Schreiner, Rick Peters, Vincent Laurence, Jon Binzen, Zachary Gaulkin, Bill Duckworth, Dennis Preston and Amie Fraser.

Jim Chiavelli
Publisher

cabinets

WILLEMSEN FOX
Newburyport, Mass.

Visage cabinet
Fir, wenge, cobalt glass
42 in. x 24 in. x 60 in.
Photo by Bill Truslow

MICHAEL HOFFER
Española, N.Mex.

Sideboard
Douglas fir, mahogany
64 in. x 20 in. x 33 in.
Photo by Jamie Hart

B.A. HARRINGTON
Somerville, Mass.

Hybrid sideboard
Quartersawn white oak,
marquetry in various veneers
58 in. x 22 in. x 40 in.
Photo by Lance Patterson

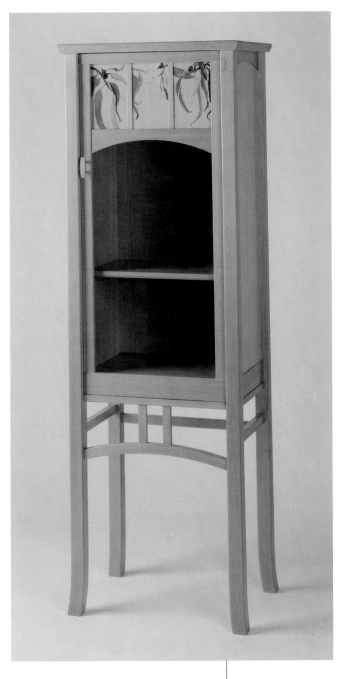

GREG ZALL
Sonoma, Calif.

Bookcase
Douglas fir
17 in. x 12 in. x 52 in.
Photo by Greg Zall

MASAHISA TSUTSUI
Nagoya-Shi, Japan

Cabinet
Oak
20 in. x 14 in. x 63 in.
Photo by Thoru Fukaya

CHRISTOPHER M. VANCE
San Diego, Calif.

"Fat Boy"
Maple, paint
30 in. x 20 in. x 42 in.
Photo by Christopher M. Vance

ANTON GERNER
East Hawthorn, Vic., Australia

Side cabinet
Tasmanian myrtle, quilted maple
veneer, gidgee
75 in. x 25 in. x 33⅓ in.
Photo by Paul Scott Photography

RICHARD L. CANTWELL
Seattle, Wash.

Found-object liquor cabinet
Cherry solid and veneer, ebony
32 in. x 8 in. x 36 in.
Photo by Adam Bujnowski

PETER NARAMORE
Kula, Hawaii

Stand
Koa veneer, solid wenge
26 in. x 16 in. x 24 in.
Photo by Peter Naramore

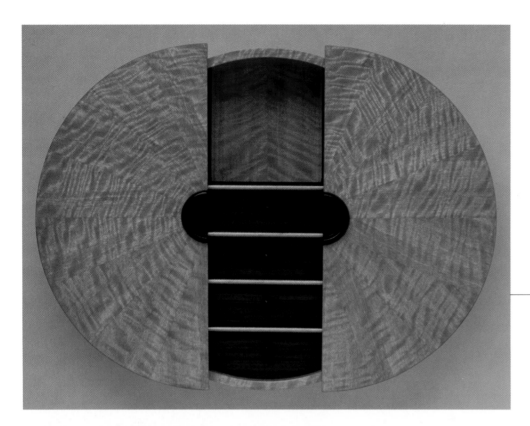

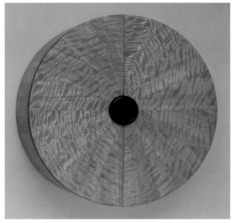

DAVID KIERNAN
Scituate, R.I.

"Sunshrine"
African satinwood, rosewood,
ebony, steel
6 in. x 18-in. dia.
Photos by Dean Powell

MARIAN YASUDA
Honolulu, Hawaii

Cabinet
Koa, Gabon ebony
30 in. x 18 in. x 49 in.
Photo by Jon DeMello

EVAN HUGHES /
EVAN HUGHES STUDIO
Brooklyn, N.Y.

Bookcase
Cherry
40 in. x 16 in. x 88 in.
Photo by Mark Gullizian
Photography

RAHI MIRAIE
Eureka, Calif.

V-front cabinet on stand
Ash, white oak,
spalted maple, olive
20 in. x 11½ in. x 56 in.
Photo by Seth Janofsky

WALTER O. JAEGER /
JAEGER & ERNST, INC.
Barboursville, Va.

Sportsman's wardrobe wall
Butternut, walnut, ebony
69 in. x 22 in. x 99 in. (center unit);
39½ in. x 22 in. x 99 in. (end units);
39 in. x 18 in. x 19½ in. (window seats)
Photos by Philip Beaurline

RAHI MIRAIE
Eureka, Calif.

Curved-doors wall cabinet
Douglas fir, yew, Alaskan
yellow cedar
18 in. x 8 in. x 22 in.
Photo by Seth Janofsky

MASON RAPAPORT
Easthampton, Mass.

Cabinet
Kevazingo, ebonized walnut
46 in. x 15 in. x 32 in.
Photo by Dean Powell

JACK RICHTER
New York, N.Y.

Vitrine
Apple ply, sapele veneer,
cast aluminum, glass
40 in. x 15 in. x 33 in.
Photo by Sean McEntee

JONATHAN P. BARAN
Adams, Mass.

Wall cabinet
Maple, applewood,
pearwood, birch
60 in. x 14 in. x 24 in.
Photo by Dean Powell

ALLAN SMITH
Hopewell, N.J.

Sideboard
Ash, black lacquered poplar
92 in. x 20 in. x 32 in.
Photo by Allan Smith

GREG ZALL
Sonoma, Calif.

"Sunflower Cabinet"
Douglas fir, satinwood,
lignum vitae, ebony
34 in. x 20 in. x 60 in.
Photos by Seth Janofsky

W. MICKEY CALLAHAN
Alexandria, Va.

Federal-style breakfront
Mahogany, crotch mahogany,
tulipwood, satinwood
80 in. x 18 in. x 90 in.
Photo by Lance Patterson

JOHN ARENSKOV
Prescott, Ariz.

Buffet
Lacewood, maple, wenge, satine
83 in. x 16 in. x 37 in.
Photo by Robert Myers

NOEL FORDE
Calgary, Alta., Canada

Display cabinet
Curly maple, glass
58 in. x 16 in. x 48 in.
Photo by Noel Forde

STEVE HOLMAN
Dorset, Vt.

"Bomboire"
Purpleheart, bubinga solids and
veneers, mahogany
52 in. x 24 in. x 92 in.
Photo by Cook Neilson

TIMOTHY COLEMAN
Greenfield, Mass.

"Three Stories"
Cherry, morado
30 in. x 12 in. x 55 in.
Photo by William Elwell

ROBBI STAPLES
Acushnet, Mass.

Sideboard
Curly, wormy serpentine maple,
bloodwood
75 in. x 19½ in. x 32 in.
Photo by John Havens Thornton

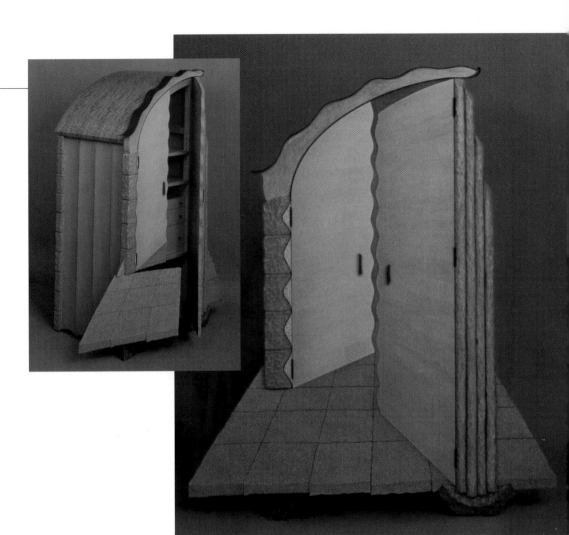

JAMIE ROBERTSON
Concord, Mass.

Media cabinet
Citrus wood, holly, purpleheart,
satinwood
51 in. x 24 in. x 63 in.
Photos by Robertson & DeRham

YUJI MORITA
Saga, Japan

Sideboard
Japanese oak
72 in. x 18 in. x 34 in.
Photo by Yoshiyuki Sakaki

M. NOELLE KHATTAB
Belmont, Mass.

"Calla Lily Cabinet"
Holly, curly maple, dyed veneers
on plywood core
17½ in. x 4 in. x 22 in.
Photo by Dean Powell

DAN MOSHEIM
Arlington, Vt.

Sideboard
Mahogany, maple, pine,
quartersawn oak
(Custom veneering by K&B
Woodworking, Cairo, N.Y.)
70 in. x 22 in. x 38 in.
Photo by Cook Neilson

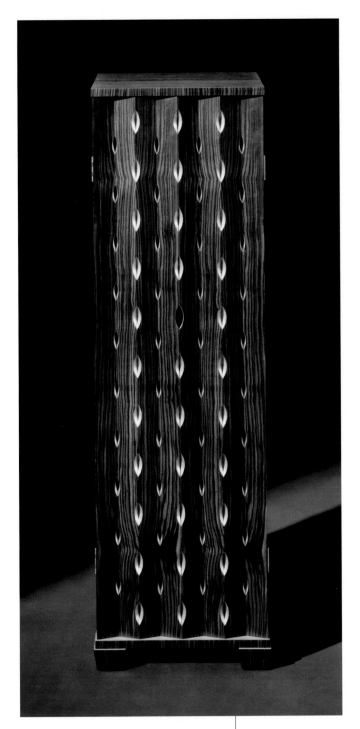

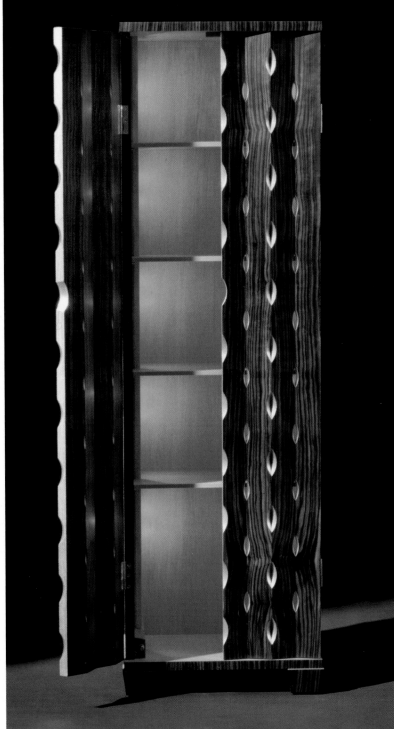

GREGG LIPTON
Cumberland, Maine

Curio cabinet
Macassar ebony, Swiss
pearwood, silver leaf
18 in. x 13 in. x 60 in.
Photos by Jeffrey Stevensen

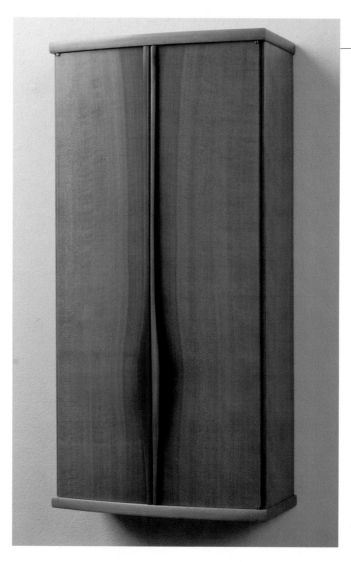

MICHAEL CARROLL
Fort Bragg, Calif.

Crystal/wine glass cabinet
Madrone
12 in. x 6 in. x 24 in.
Photo by Anne Knudsen

DAVID J. MARKS
Santa Rosa, Calif.

Buffet
Quilted maple, maple, ebony,
wenge, Honduras mahogany
72 in. x 20 in. x 36 in.
Photos by Don Russel

GARY ROGOWSKI
Portland, Ore.

"Tansu"
Honduras mahogany,
pomele sapele, ebony
67 in. x 22 in. x 29 in.
Photo by Phil Harris

HENRY R. LINDER, JR.
Roseville, Minn.

Drinks cabinet
Quartersawn East Indian
rosewood veneer, Cuban
mahogany, rosewood, Corian
36 in. x 18 in. x 42 in.
Photo by Chris Schafer

FRANK POLLARO
E. Orange, N.J.

"Ruhlmann-Grande
Cannelée À Redents"
Amboyna burl, faux ivory
66 in. x 20 in. x 34 in.
Photo by Vinnie Strange

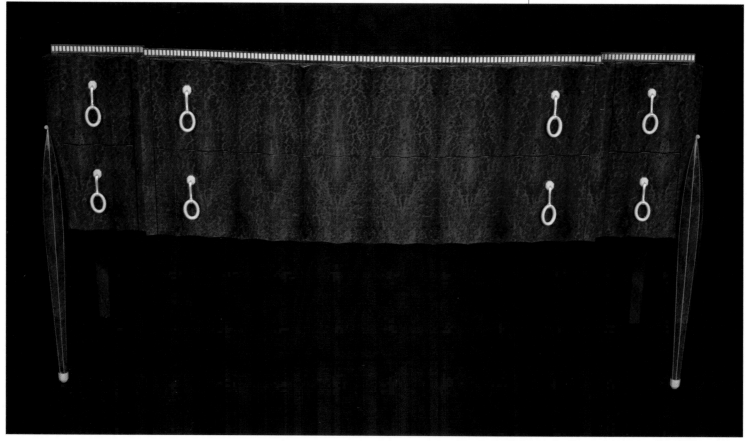

ROBIN GREENWOOD
Toronto, Ont., Canada

CD/cassette cabinet
Cherry, cherry veneer, walnut,
Baltic birch plywood
40 in. x 25 in. x 28 in.
Photo by Sherman Laws

MARK NATHENSON
Macedon, N.Y.

"Coral Reef Buffet"
Figured ash, bocote, satinwood,
ebony, painted basswood
41½ in. x 20 in. x 43 in.
Photo by Daniel Neuberger

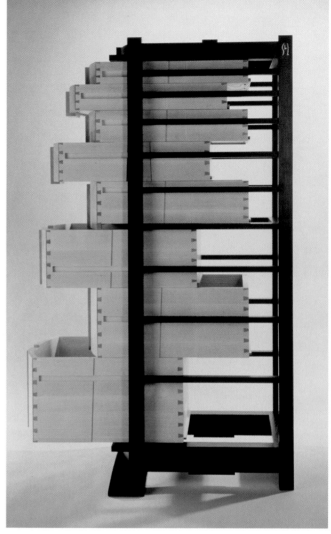

CHRISTOPH NEANDER
Providence, R.I.

"Column of Drawers"
Northern white ash
23 in. x 23 in. x 58 in.
Photos by James Beards

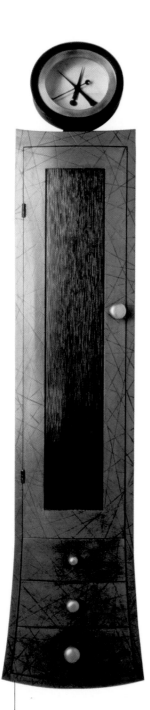

CHRISTOPHER M. VANCE
San Diego, Calif.

"All Tied Up"
Maple, gold leaf, milk paint
8 in. x 12 in. x 48 in.
Photo by Christopher M. Vance

RENE ALMON
San Leandro, Calif.

"Showcase on a Stand"
European cherry, teak, cypress
21 in. x 12 in. x 59 in.
Photo by Seth Janofsky

25

MARK NATHENSON
Macedon, N.Y.

"Tai Pan Cabinet"
Ebonized cherry, painted
basswood
24½ in. x 19¼ in. x 64 in.
Photo by Neuberger/Koft

EVAN HUGHES /
EVAN HUGHES STUDIO
Brooklyn, N.Y.

Bureau
Satinwood, maple, steel
81 in. x 23 in. x 32 in.
Photo by Beth Phillips
Photography

TIMOTHY COLEMAN
Greenfield, Mass.

Fluted cabinet
White oak, maple
23 in. x 13 in. x 49 in.
Photo by David Ryan

chairs & benches

ROD HOUSTON
Ilfeld, N.Mex.

Rocker
Walnut
52 in. x 24 in. x 48 in.
Photo by Herbert Lotz

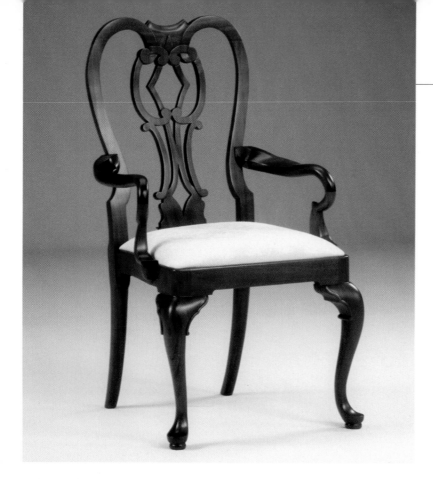

CARLTON B. CRAIG
Bassett, Va.

Dining host chair
Mahogany
22 in. x 19 in. x 39¼ in.
Photo by Mike Arnold

GEOFFREY NODEN
Trenton, N.J.

Arched-top chair
Walnut, satinwood
20 in. x 22 in. x 54 in.
Photos by Geoffrey Noden

JAMES CASEBOLT
Santa Cruz, Calif.

"Sitz Machine"
Honduras mahogany,
Gabon ebony
37 in. x 27 in. x 36¾ in.
Photo by Dan Quijano

MARC RICHARDSON
Montreal, Que., Canada

Dining chair
Mahogany, ebony
18 in. x 20½ in. x 56 in.
Photo by Roger Thibault

RICHARD PRISCO
Savannah, Ga.

Chaise
Mahogany
74 in. x 27 in. x 39 in.
Photo by Rick Shannon

DOUGLAS FINKEL
Richmond, Va.

Chair
Walnut
18 in. x 25 in. x 42 in.
Photo by Arthur Probst

YANG JUN KWON
San Diego, Calif.

"Home of Morning Calm"
Ash, mahogany
19½ in. x 20 in. x 53 in.
Photo by Ken Von Schlegall

MARK J. SPADAFORA
Rochester, N.Y.

Chair
Purpleheart, maple,
English curly maple
18 in. x 21½ in. x 31½ in.
Photo by Chris Kay

JAY BONAVENTURA
Brisbane, Australia

Dining chair
Black wattle, silver ash, ebony
18 in. x 18 in. x 37¾ in.
Photos by Profile Photographics

JOHN PAYNE
San Jose, Calif.
Chair
Maple, bubinga
24 in. x 22 in. x 52 in.
Photo by Curtis Fukuda

JOHN and CAROLYN
GREW-SHERIDAN
San Francisco, Calif.
"C/Y"
Sustained-yield Belize mahogany
22 in. x 20 in. x 36 in.
Photo by Schopplein Studio

JANICE C. SMITH
Lawrence, Kans.
"Lateen"
Sapele pomele manufactured
veneer
66 in. x 24 in. x 38 in.
Photo by Reuben P. Wade

ROBERT DIEMERT
Dundas, Ont., Canada

Metro hall chair
Cherry, hand-dyed and woven
fabric by Kathleen Morris
24 in. x 24 in. x 35 in.
Photo by Jeremy Jones

THOMAS HUGH STANGELAND
Seattle, Wash.

Greene & Greene armchair
Sustained-yield mahogany,
Ebon-X
24 in. x 24 in. x 34 in.
Photo by Gregg Krogstad

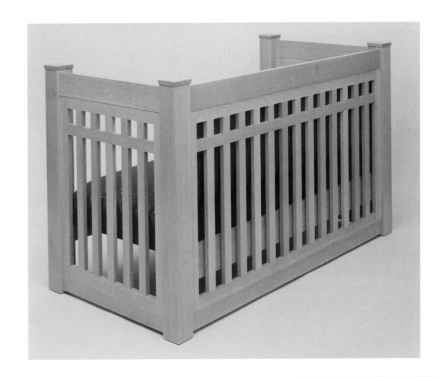

JUDITH HANSON and
B.A. HARRINGTON
Somerville, Mass.

Box settle
Quartersawn white oak,
marquetry in various veneers
59 in. x 30 in. x 37 in.
Photos by Lance Patterson

STEPHEN HULTBERG
Seattle, Wash.

Chair
Bubinga
25 in. x 21 in. x 38½ in.
Photo by John Currie

ROB GARTZKA and
KATHIE JOHNSON
Urbana, Ohio

"Red Clay Garden"
Maple, poplar, Baltic birch,
alkyd oil paint, leather
58 in. x 27 in. x 41 in.
Photos by Tony Walsh

ROBERT E.S. TROUTMAN
Crestone, Colo.

"Neo-Rustic One-Armed Chair"
Mountain maple, cattail
27 in. x 27 in. x 59 in.
Photo by J.D. Marston

MARTIN SIMPSON
Providence, R.I.

"Three's Company"
Bleached maple, bleached wenge
66 in. x 29 in. x 42 in.
Photo by Mark Johnston

CHRIS RICE
Harwinton, Conn.

Occasional chair
Walnut, ebony, leather
18 in. x 18 in. x 40 in.
Photo by Adam Bartowski

MASON RAPAPORT
Easthampton, Mass.

Dining chair
Curly maple, walnut
23½ in. x 21 in. x 42 in.
Photo by Dean Powell

DAVID P. LEIGHLY
Rochester, Minn.

Drafting chair
African padauk, walnut
20 in. x 18 in. x 44 in.
Photo by Greg Larson

JEFFREY GREENE
Doylestown, Pa.

"Flame Chair"
Bolivian rosewood,
African wenge
23 in. x 17 in. x 55 in.
Photo by Randyl Bye

MICHAEL STERLING
Chico, Calif.

Pair of chairs
Claro walnut, ebony,
putumuju (slats, left chair)
19½ in. x 20½ in. x 54 in.
Photo by Jeff Teeter

RUSSELL BALDON
San Diego, Calif.

Dining room chair
Ash, steel
20 in. x 22 in. x 28 in.
Photo by Russell Baldon

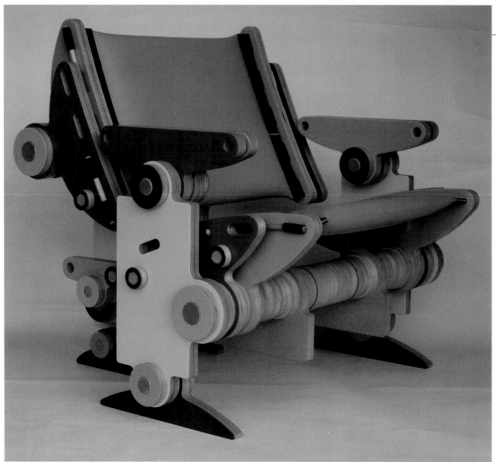

KENNETH SMYTHE
Berkeley, Calif.

"Originalitas Deliberata I"
Finnish birch laminate
30 in. x 34 in. x 33 in.
Photo by Kenneth Smythe

CRAIG ERNST /
JAEGER & ERNST, INC.
Barboursville, Va.

Rocking chair
Cherry, maple
42 in. x 24 in. x 42 in.
Photo by Philip Beaurline

BARRY R. YAVENER
Buffalo, N.Y.

"Under the Canopy"
Yucatan machech
40 in. x 36 in. x 36 in. (closed);
40 in. x 36 in. x 78 in. (open)
Photos by Tom Loonan

PHILLIP A. STAFFORD
Lakeland, Tenn.

Rocker
Maple, hickory, black lacquer
31 in. x 25 in. x 42 in.
Photo by Phillip A. Stafford

MASAHISA TSUTSUI
Nagoya-Shi, Japan

"Mikado"
Zelkova
39 in. x 28 in. x 36 in.
Photo by Thoru Fukaya

MARK CASSEL GRABLE
Indianapolis, Ind.

"Cloud Chair"
Walnut
57 in. x 24 in. x 34 in.
Photo by Tom Ransburg

JEFF MILLER
Chicago, Ill.

"Stained Glass Chairs"
Cherry, ebony
20 in. x 21 in. x 44 in.
Photo by Stuart Block

B.A. HARRINGTON
Somerville, Mass.

Federal-inspired side chair
Cherry, ebony, madrone burl
veneer
19 in. x 19½ in. x 35 in.
Photo by Lance Patterson

ROBERT MARCH
Princeton, Mass.

Bench
Curly maple, purpleheart
42 in. x 16 in. x 16 in.
Photo by Dean Powell

THOMAS STARBUCK STOCKTON
Petaluma, Calif.

Arts and Crafts settle
Cherry, ebony, sterling silver
72 in. x 36 in. x 30 in.
Photo by Matt Prince

KEVIN GRAY
Fruitvale, Idaho

Free-arm rocker
Walnut, ebonized walnut
46 in. x 25 in. x 45 in.
Photo by Kevin Gray

tables

JOHN C. MOTSIS
Boston, Mass.

Card table
Mahogany, poplar, veneers of
fiddleback, mahogany, rosewood,
holly, ebonized holly
35 in. x 18 in. x 29 in.
Photo by Lance Patterson

CLIFFORD COLLEY
Marshfield, Mass.

Card table
Cherry, poplar
39½ in. x 41½ in. x 29¼ in. (open);
39½ in. x 20¾ in. x 30 in. (closed)
Photo by Lance Patterson

KIM SCHMAHMANN
Cambridge, Mass.

Global vernacular side tables
Basswood, moabi and
maple veneers
24 in. x 24 in. x 28 in.
Photo by Lance Patterson

WILLIAM HOWARD
West Hatfield, Mass.

Entryway table
Bird's-eye maple, dyed maple,
ebony
43½ in. x 13½ in. x 33 in.
Photo by Dean Powell

ROBERT KOPF
Walnut Cove, N.C.

Hanes table
Curly maple, ebonized ash
57 in. x 17 in. x 35 in.
Photo by Jackson Smith

ANDREW McINNES
Newburyport, Mass.

William & Mary dressing table
Walnut, walnut veneer, birch,
poplar, basswood, soft maple
36 in. x 21 in. x 30 in.
Photo by Lance Patterson

JAMIE ROBERTSON
Concord, Mass.

"Julia's Dog"
East Indian rosewood,
pau amarillo
72 in. x 20 in. x 35 in.
Photo by Robertson & DeRham

JOHN W. GOFF
San Diego, Calif.

Chippendale-style game table
Honduran mahogany, baize
33 in. x 33 in. x 27½ in. (open);
33 in. x 16½ in. x 27½ in. (closed)
Photos by Kevin Halle

KAREN E. BAISCH
Ipswich, Mass.

Federal-period side table
Mahogany crotch veneer,
mahogany, cocobolo, maple
37 in. x 18 in. x 28 in.
Photo by Lance Patterson

IVY DIXON
Portland, Ore.

Table
Cherry, marble, stainless steel, glass
24 in. x 23½ in. x 25⅜ in. x 17½-in. dia.
Photo by Ivy Dixon

CHARLES GRUBB
Bryn Athyn, Pa.

"Wacky Legs"
Poplar, sycamore
20 in. x 20 in. x 17 in.
Photo by Michael Price

JEFF JOHNSON
Poughkeepsie, N.Y.

Coffee table
Quilted maple, glass
42 in. x 18 in. x 17 in.
Photo by Al Nowak

ROBERT DIEMERT
Dundas, Ont., Canada

Tripod table
East Indian rosewood
22 in. x 22-in. dia.
Photo by Jeremy Jones

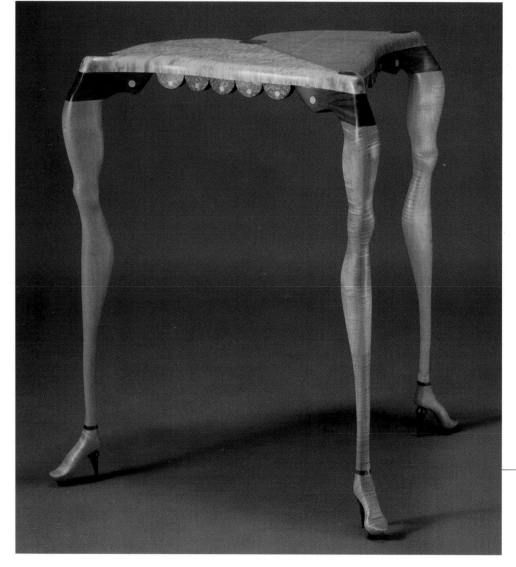

ROBERT DIEMERT
Dundas, Ont., Canada

End tables/cabinets
Bubinga, Macassar ebony
26 in. x 22 in. x 22 in.
Photo by Jeremy Jones

DALE LEWIS
Calera, Ala.

"Norma Jean, You're Still Queen"
Bird's-eye maple, bubinga, dyed
curly maple, lacewood,
satinwood
24 in. x 22 in. x 31 in.
Photo by Dale Lewis

JOSEPH BREWER
Camden, Maine

Side table
Mahogany, redwood burl
23 in. x 15 in. x 22 in.
Photo by William Thuss

COLIN REID
Oakland, Calif.

"Okavango Series" coffee table
Quilted mahogany, glass
15 in. x 42-in. dia.
Photo by Lee Fatherree

MICHAEL CULLEN
Petaluma, Calif.

Wankel/side table
Mahogany, glass
22 in. x 24-in. dia.
Photo by Don Russel

THOMAS STARBUCK STOCKTON
Petaluma, Calif.

Dining table
Mahogany, ebony, abalone
78 in. x 42 in. x 29 in.
Photo by Matt Prince

BRETT ALLEN HESSER
San Diego, Calif.

Coffee table
Purpleheart, Sri Lankan
satinwood, maple
18 in. x 34-in. dia.
Photos by Birdie Carter
Photography

JIM WOLNOSKY
Bath, Mich.

Hall table
Bird's-eye maple, purpleheart,
ebonized walnut
52 in. x 7 in. x 29½ in.
Photo by Jim Wolnosky

JONATHAN P. BARAN
Adams, Mass.

Hall table
Walnut, curly maple,
zebrawood veneer
40 in. x 16 in. x 34 in.
Photo by Dean Powell

DENNIS YOUNG
Nagano-Ken, Japan

Dining table with chairs
Claro walnut
28 in. x 48-in. dia.
Photo by Studio White

DENNIS L. MEADOR
Cookeville, Tenn.

Table
Cherry, maple, Plexiglas
18 in. x 12 in. x 18 in.
Photo by John Lucas

JEFF MILLER
Chicago, Ill.

"Spider Handkerchief Table"
Maple, bird's-eye maple,
purpleheart
45¼ in. x 23½ in. x 30 in.
Photo by Stuart Block

SARAH McCREA
Clyde, N.C.

Fan table
White oak
36 in. x 36 in. x 30 in.
Photo by Robert Gibson

RICK NORRANDER
Wood Village, Ore.

Dining table
Maple, tulipwood, ebony,
bloodwood, purpleheart
74 in. x 48 in. x 29 in.
Photo by Studio 3 Inc.

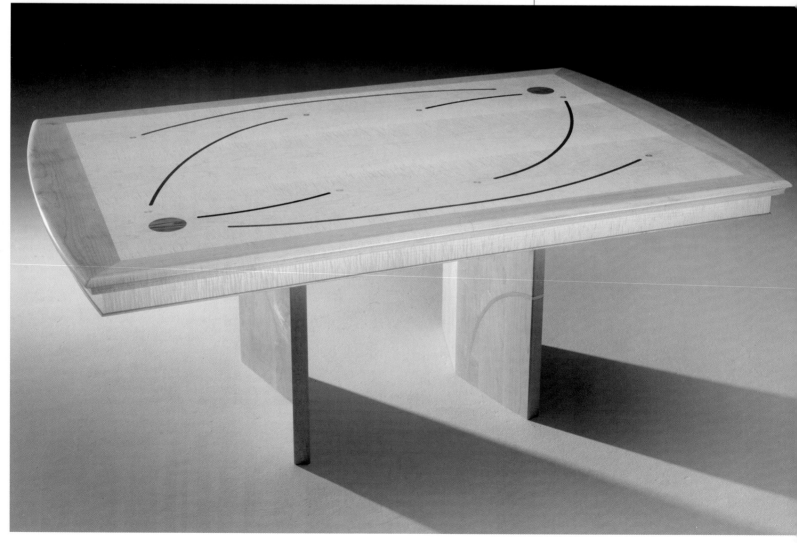

JUDITH P. HANSON
Boston, Mass.

Sheraton work table
Mahogany, bird's-eye maple,
cocobolo, poplar
18 in. x 17 in. x 27½ in.
Photo by Lance Patterson

GRADY MATHEWS
Brier, Wash.

Lattice coffee table
Eastern maple, padauk
44 in. x 32 in. x 17 in.
Photo by Gregg Krogstad

JOHN BARTOSH
Malden, Mass.

Philadelphia Chippendale
tea table
South American mahogany
36 in. x 19 in. x 34 in.
Photo by Lance Patterson

RICHARD L. CANTWELL
Seattle, Wash.

"The Difficult Whole"
Mahogany, aluminum, silver leaf
52 in. x 19 in. x 31 in.
Photo by Mike Richter

SEAN McENTEE
Elmsford, N.Y.

"Demi-Loon/Dysfunctional
Furniture Series"
Mahogany, peroba rosa,
beech ply
48 in. x 15 in. x 38 in.
Photo by Sean McEntee

CHRIS GANS
Tucson, Ariz.

Dining table with chairs
Lacewood, wenge,
aluminum, glass
84 in. x 42 in. x 29 in.
Photo by Ray Manley Studio

M. ALEXANDER MALEK
Glendale, Colo.

"Lydia"
Lacewood, wenge, aluminum,
wire, glass
20 in. x 20 in. x 24 in.
Photo by B. Kende

JOHN P. McCORMACK
Providence, R.I.

Trestle table
Maple
80 in. x 40 in. x 30 in.
Photo by Mitch Rice Photography

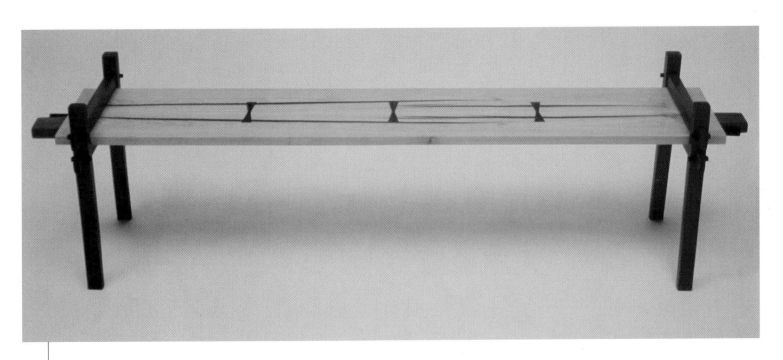

DANIEL KAGAY
Florence, Tex.

"Sushi, Anyone?"
Walnut, poplar, ebony
48 in. x 12 in. x 16 in.
Photo by Charlie Guerrero

DEREK S. DAVIS
Boulder, Colo.

"Cloisters Table"
Brazilian rosewood, wenge,
purpleheart, bird's-eye maple
49 in. x 15 in. x 30 in.
Photo by Michael Bush

B. DASS
Aurora, Ont., Canada

Coffee table
Purpleheart, bird's-eye maple, ebony
41 in. x 18 in. x 17 in.
Photo by Joseph Camilleri

TED HARLAN
Louisville, Ky.

Living tables
Cherry, bronze
66 in. x 27 in. x 17 in.
Photo by Phil Cooley

RICHARD PRISCO
Savannah, Ga.

"Little Ash Table"
Ash, glass, wire
36 in. x 18 in. x 39 in.
Photo by Rick Shannon

MIKE FLANAGAN
Petaluma, Calif.

"Hall Table #2"
Macore, wenge, ebony
46 in. x 16 in. x 34 in.
Photo by Don Russel

DUNCAN W. GOWDY
La Mesa, Calif.

"Hungry"
Poplar, basswood
52 in. x 30 in. x 18 in.
Photos by John Horner

ROGER HEITZMAN
Scotts Valley, Calif.

Dining table
Figured anegre, maple, wenge
29½ in. x 53-in. dia.
Photo by Roger Heitzman

GRAHAM CAMPBELL
Smithville, Tenn.

"#100 Hall Table"
Ash, MDF
48 in. x 16 in. x 36 in.
Photo by John Lucas

DAVID KIERNAN
Scituate, R.I.

Hall table
Black lacquered maple, sterling
silver inlay, textured mahogany
72 in. x 12 in. x 36 in.
Photo by Dean Powell

DIANE STANTON
Atlanta, Ga.

Hall table
MDF, steel
35 in. x 15 in. x 35 in.
Photo by Diane Stanton

ROBERT HACKER
Olney, Md.

Demilune
Walnut, tiger maple, maple inlay
59 in. x 21 in. x 30 in.
Photo by Ellen Cohan

W. CURTIS JOHNSON
Corvallis, Ore.

Sofa/hall table
White oak, black
lacquered walnut
56 in. x 14 in. x 28 in.
Photo by W. Curtis Johnson

PAUL SCHÜRCH
Santa Barbara, Calif.

Small game table
Walnut, laurel, pollard ash,
tulipwood, padauk, mansonia,
maple, purpleheart, pearwood,
narranga, poplar, boxwood, black
pearwood, Baltic birch
24½ in. x 24½ in. x 29 in.
Photo by Wayne McCall

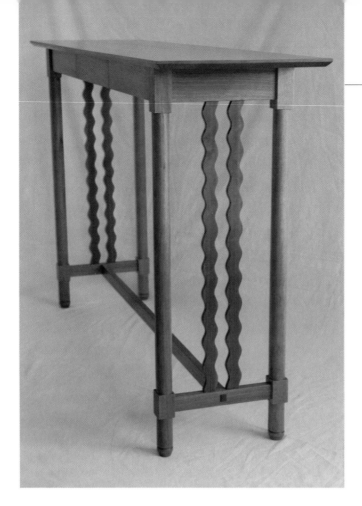

LEO SADLEK
Neerim, South Vic., Australia

Hall table
Mahogany, red iron bark
51 in. x 16 in. x 36 in.
Photo by Leo Sadlek

MICHAEL PURYEAR
New York, N.Y.

Table
Ash, wenge
52 in. x 18 in. x 32 in.
Photo by Sarah Wells

SABIHA MUJTABA
Atlanta, Ga.

"A Basket of Snakes"
Curly maple, zebrawood, wenge,
padauk, purpleheart, rope
72 in. x 42 in. x 30 in.
Photo by Kurt Fisher

JEFFREY ATWOOD GIBSON
Boston, Mass.

Corner table
Solid and veneer crotch
mahogany, poplar, holly inlay
28 in. x 18 in. x 33 in.
Photo by Lance Patterson

PETER SHEPARD
W. Concord, Mass.

Conference table
Cherry, rosewood
106 in. x 46 in. x 29 in.
Photo by Dean Powell

WILLIAM KEYSER
Victor, N.Y.

Conference table
Solid white oak, curly white
oak veneer, wenge
30 in. x 42-in. dia.
Photo by David Leveille/
Northlight Studios

SCOTT HAUSMANN
Brattleboro, Vt.

Pedestal table
Lacewood, ebonized cherry
22 in. x 29-in. dia.
Photo by Scott Hausmann

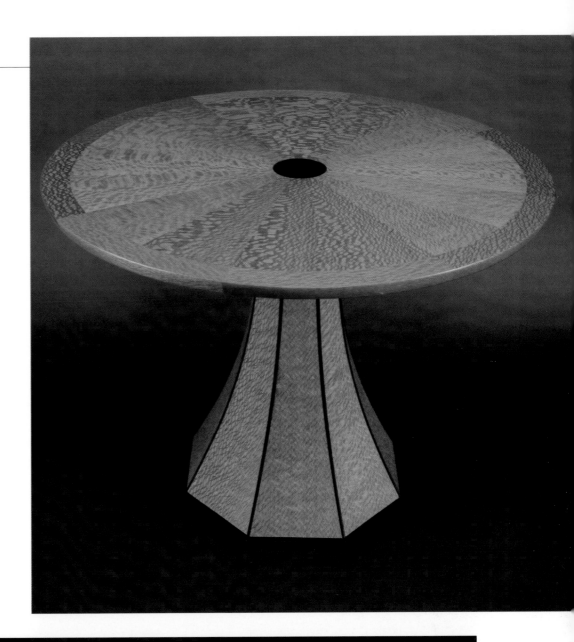

JOHN MICHAEL PIERSON
Lemon Grove, Calif.

"Ribbon Coffee Table"
Poplar, avodire, glass
60 in. x 28 in. x 17 in.
Photo by Dan Otto

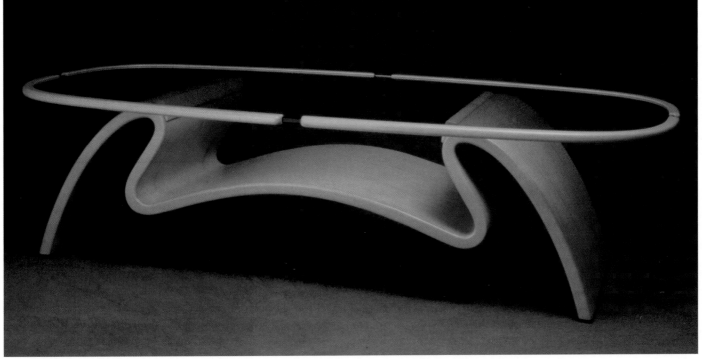

boxes & chests

KEITH SARGENT CORNELL
Cambridge, Mass.

"Chest on Chest on Chest"
Cherry, Carpathian elm burl, holly
44 in. x 22 in. x 64 in.
Photo by Lance Patterson

RANDY COOK
Long Beach, Wash.

"Corner Leg Box"
Yew, rosewood, apple ply
4½ in. x 4½ in. x 9 in.
Photo by George Post

CHRISTIAN BURCHARD
Ashland, Ore.

Chest of drawers
Black walnut, madrone,
rosewood, oak, brass
84 in. x 24 in. x 28 in.
Photo by Robert Jaffe

KIP CHRISTENSEN
Springville, Vt.

Pencil boxes
Bird's-eye maple, white oak,
spalted pecan, black walnut,
mistletoe-infested claro walnut
8 in. x 4 in. x 2½ in.
Photo by Glenn Anderson

ADAM CHESIS
Pittsford, N.Y.

Chest of drawers
Mahogany, red oak
36 in. x 18 in. x 60 in.
Photo by Adam Bujnowski

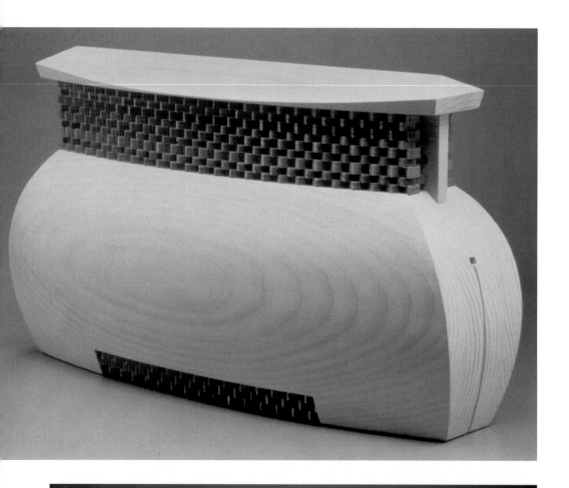

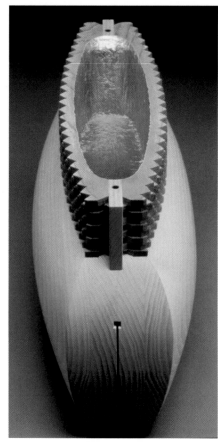

PETER A. CHRISMAN
Tucson, Ariz.

Dresser
Bird's-eye maple, wenge, pewter
42 in. x 20 in. x 38 in.
Photo by Tom Eglin

RICHARD TANNEN
Honeoye Falls, N.Y.

"Reliquary III"
Bleached, dyed ash, gold leaf
15 in. x 4½ in. x 8 in.
Photos by Rick Shannon

CHRISTOPH NEANDER
Providence, R.I.

"Soothing the Blues"
Eastern white pine, maple,
cedar, acrylic paint
42 in. x 20 in. x 21 in.
Photo by James Beards

STEVEN M. WHITE
Berkeley, Calif.

Jewelry chest
Padauk, maple, ebony
24 in. x 15 in. x 42 in.
Photo by Steven M. White

JAMIE ROBERTSON
Concord, Mass.

Tall ripple chest
African satinwood, dyed poplar
33 in. x 23 in. x 48 in.
Photo by Robertson & DeRham

BRETT ALLEN HESSER
San Diego, Calif.

Chest of drawers
Bubinga, ebony, maple
72 in. x 20 in. x 36 in.
Photo by Birdie Carter
Photography

JO RUSKIN ROESSLER
Croton, N.Y.

Jewelry box
Red oak, mahogany,
maple, rice paper
14 in. x 11 in. x 23 in.
Photo by Jo Ruskin Roessler

NIKOLAUS MELLER
Boston, Mass.

"North Bennet Street
School Toolbox"
Cherry, poplar, ebony
32 in. x 20 in. x 17 in.
Photo by Lance Patterson

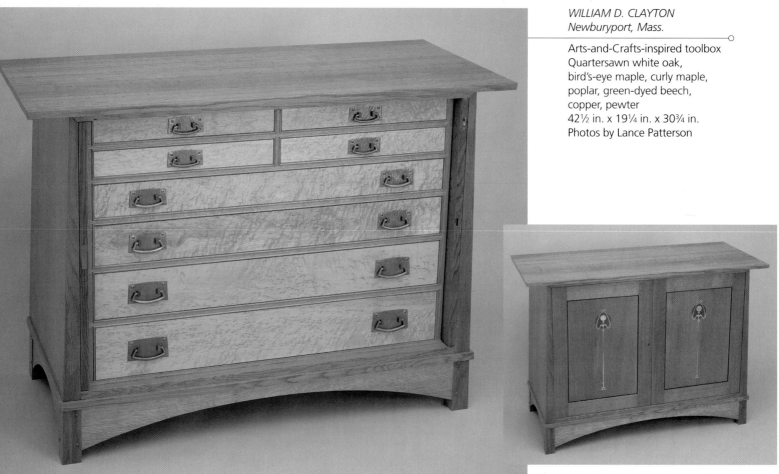

WILLIAM D. CLAYTON
Newburyport, Mass.

Arts-and-Crafts-inspired toolbox
Quartersawn white oak,
bird's-eye maple, curly maple,
poplar, green-dyed beech,
copper, pewter
42½ in. x 19¼ in. x 30¾ in.
Photos by Lance Patterson

THOMAS HUGH STANGELAND
Seattle, Wash.

Jewelry chest
Satinwood, ebony, brass
20 in. x 10 in. x 15 in.
Photo by Thomas Hugh
Stangeland

LANCE PATTERSON
Boston, Mass.

Queen Anne highboy
Curly maple
42 in. x 23 in. x 78 in.
Photo by Lance Patterson

JIM QUINSEY
Whitehorse, Yukon, Canada

Jewelry box
Yellow cedar, white oak
15¾ in. x 7⅞ in. x 6⅝ in.
Photos by Robin Armour

MARIAN YASUDA
Honolulu, Hawaii

Chest of drawers
Silky oak, eucalyptus robusta,
glass
38 in. x 22 in. x 56 in.
Photo by Tom Gibson

DEWEY GARRETT
Livermore, Calif.

Harlequin box
Oak, padauk
5 in. x 10½-in. dia.
Photo by Jim Ferreira

ANTON GERNER
East Hawthorn, Vic., Australia

Chest of drawers
Figured Tasmanian myrtle,
fiddleback blackwood,
celery top pine, gidgee
50 in. x 25 in. x 62½ in.
Photo by Paul Scott Photography

ARTIE F. TABRIZI
Woodland Hills, Calif.

Chest of drawers
Bubinga, birch, cherry, metal
laminate, Baltic birch
18 in. x 31 in. x 44 in.
Photo by Paul Jonason
Photography

ARVID LYONS
Clarkston, Wash.

Grain-worn blanket chest
Reclaimed barn boards (fir and
pine), spalted maple
38 in. x 16 in. x 19 in.
Photo by Ryan McGuire

PETER SHEPARD
W. Concord, Mass.

Silver hall chest
Curly maple, ebony
28 in. x 18 in. x 34 in.
Photo by Dean Powell

JOHN BARTOSH
Malden, Mass.

Tool chest
Mahogany, curly maple,
ebonized maple
42 in. x 21 in. x 35 in.
Photos by Lance Patterson

PETER S. TURNER /
ALCYON WOODWORKS
Portland, Maine

Jewelry box
Cherry, granadillo
19 in. x 7½ in. x 7 in.
Photo by Seth Hanson

BRIAN BEARD
Sweet Home, Ore.

Queen Anne lowboy
Waferwood, Masonite
31 in. x 20 in. x 30 in.
Photo by Craig Iwo

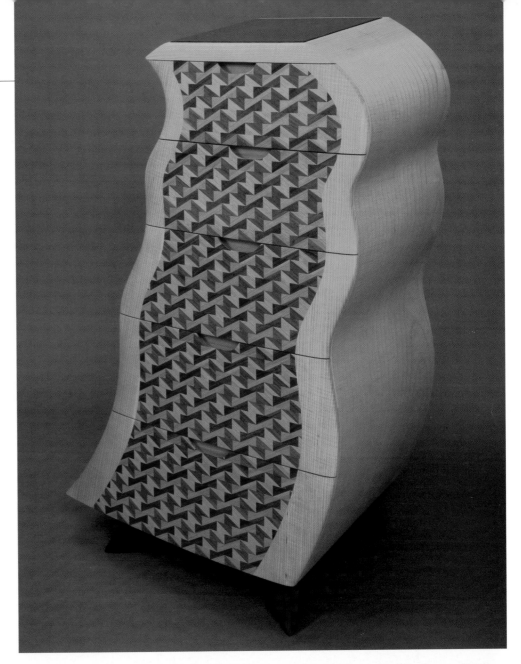

DEREK S. DAVIS
Boulder, Colo.

"Mrs. Frump's Night Out"
Curly ash, hickory, koa
30 in. x 17 in. x 45 in.
Photo by Michael Bush

GEOFFREY D. WARNER
Exeter, R.I.

"Fish Chest"
Curly maple, red cedar, paint
41 in. x 19 in. x 20 in.
Photo by James Beards

COURTNEY FAIR
Providence, R.I.

Chest
White oak, steel, Plexiglas
18 in. x 16 in. x 60 in.
Photo by Roger Schriber

W. MICKEY CALLAHAN
Alexandria, Va.

Blanket chest
Mahogany, sapele, holly,
ebony, satinwood
40 in. x 18 in. x 24 in.
Photo by Lance Patterson

DAN MOSHEIM
Arlington, Vt.

Tall tapered chest
Curly maple, redwood, lacewood,
mahogany, quartersawn oak,
pine, pau ferro
42 in. x 22 in. x 78 in.
Photo by Cook Neilson

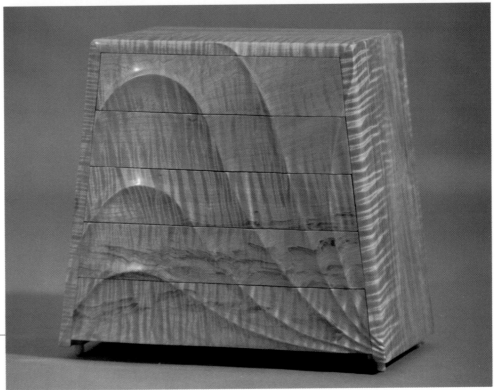

CHRISTOPHER KUNKLE
Fayetteville, Ark.

"Wave" jewelry box
Curly maple
9 in. x 6 in. x 10 in.
Photo by Christopher Kunkle

desks

ANTHONY KAHN
Arcata, Calif.

Standing desk and tripod stool
California walnut, wenge
42 in. x 30 in. x 48 in.
Photo by J. Patrick Cudahy

ARNO BRIEHL
Ravensburg, Germany

Writing desk
European ash, grained ash
48 in. x 25¼ in. x 40¼ in.
Photos by Uwe Gartze

MICHAEL CULLEN
Petaluma, Calif.

Moon desk
Pernanbuco, satinwood,
ebonized mahogany, fino, ebony
26 in. x 20 in. x 38 in.
Photo by Dean Powell

SCOTT E. ARMSTRONG
Powell, Wyo.

Gambrel writing table and stool
Maple, mahogany
48 in. x 17 in. x 30 in.
Photo by Elijah Cobb

SHELLEY FLANAGAN
San Leandro, Calif.

Desk and chair
European cherry, maple, olivewood
36½ in. x 22 in. x 29½ in.
Photo by Tom Liden

WILLEMSEN FOX
Newburyport, Mass.

Writing desk
Curly cherry, copper leaf,
paint, glass
60 in. x 30 in. x 30 in.
Photo by Bill Truslow

DANIEL S. NEWMAN
Ann Arbor, Mich.

Writing desk
Quilted mahogany, Gabon ebony,
bird's-eye maple
58 in. x 27½ in. x 29 in.
Photos by Mark Orr

LARRY FAGAN
Prescott, Ariz.

Desk
Bird's-eye maple, mahogany
53 in. x 26 in. x 29 in.
Photos by Larry Fagan

GAVIN O'GRADY
San Diego, Calif.

Desk and chair
Painted birch, plywood, leather
33 in. x 21 in. x 53 in.
Photos by Ken Von Schlegell

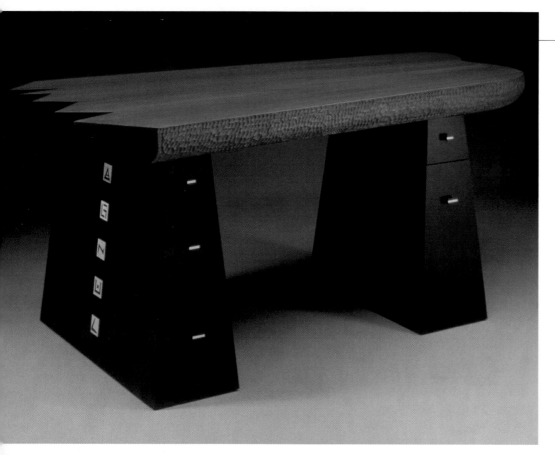

DAVID KIERNAN
Scituate, R.I.

"Megalith"
Mahogany, dyed black costello,
ebony, sterling silver inlay
66 in. x 32 in. x 30 in.
Photo by Dean Powell

MARC RICHARDSON
Montreal, Que., Canada

Desk
Cherry, wenge
60 in. x 32 in. x 29 in.
Photo by Roger Thibault

RICK ALLYN
Twin Falls, Idaho

Writing desk
Mahogany, pearwood,
maple, cocobolo
47 in. x 23 in. x 30 in.
Photo by Rick Allyn

JOHN GLENDINNING
Kitchener, Ont., Canada

Writing table and chair
Mahogany, bird's-eye maple,
maple, dyed black boxwood
veneer
48 in. x 24 in. x 29 in.
Photo by John Glendinning

GREGG LIPTON
Cumberland, Maine

"Marilyn"
Indian satinwood,
bee's-wing maple
56 in. x 28 in. x 57 in.
Photo by Stretch Tuemmler

MICHAEL CARROLL
Fort Bragg, Calif.

Writing desk
California walnut, maple,
pecan inlay
59 in. x 34 in. x 30½ in.
Photo by Seth Janofsky

ROGER HEITZMAN
Scotts Valley, Calif.

Desk and chair
Tiger maple, curly sycamore,
wenge
62 in. x 24 in. x 30 in.
Photo by Roger Heitzman

RAY KELSO / TREEBEARD DESIGNS, INC.
Collegeville, Pa.

Writing table
Curly cherry, walnut, calfskin
48 in. x 18 in. x 30 in.
Photos by Tom Crane

DENNIS YOUNG
Nagano-Ken, Japan

Desk for tatami room
Purpleheart, ebony
31 in. x 14½ in. x 13½ in.
Photo by Studio White

WARREN A. MAY
Berea, Ky.

Kentucky secretary bookcase
Walnut
40½ in. x 21 in. x 84 in.
Photos by Dave Robertson

STEPHEN D. HENDRY
Middlesex, England

"Flight of Fancy"
Sycamore, ebony
41¾ in. x 23⅜ in. x 29 in.
Photo by Stephen D. Hendry

ALEX ROSKIN
Williamsport, Pa.

Desk
Cherry, ash, Ebon-X
65½ in. x 32 in. x 31 in.
Photos by The Terry Wild Studio

JOEL LIEBMAN
Hadley, Mass.

Desk and chair
Maple, cherry
48 in. x 35 in. x 29 in.
Photo by Joel Liebman

WILLIAM KEYSER
Victor, N.Y.

Desk
Solid white oak, curly white oak
veneer, wenge
72 in. x 36 in. x 30 in.
Photo by David Leveille/
Northlight Studios

JOHN and CAROLYN
GREW-SHERIDAN
San Francisco, Calif.

Corvin desk
Granadillo, alder, maple,
copper, plastic laminate
72 in. x 36 in. x 29 in.
Photo by Schopplein Studio

TIMOTHY COLEMAN
Greenfield, Mass.

Desk and chair
Pearwood, Australian silky oak
42 in. x 22 in. x 30 in.
Photos by David Ryan

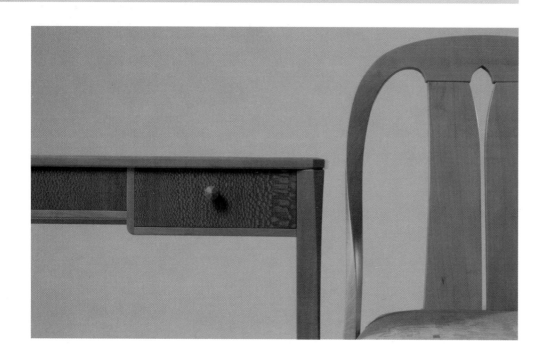

ANDREW JACOBSON
Petaluma, Calif.

Writing desk
Quilted mahogany,
mahogany, ebony
63 in. x 34 in. x 29 in.
Photo by Dennis Anderson

beds & furnishings

DEAN JACKSON and
SIGGI BÜHLER
Toronto, Ont., Canada

"The Ballroom Bar"
Oak, marble
8 ft. x 18-ft. dia.
Photo by Pam Carnell

SAMUEL DOLEMAN
Richmond, Calif.

Nightstand
Padauk
15 in. x 15 in. x 26 in.
Photo by Samuel Doleman

MARIAN YASUDA
Honolulu, Hawaii

Vanity with mirror
Koa, brass
56 in. x 18 in. x 50 in.
Photo by Tom Gibson

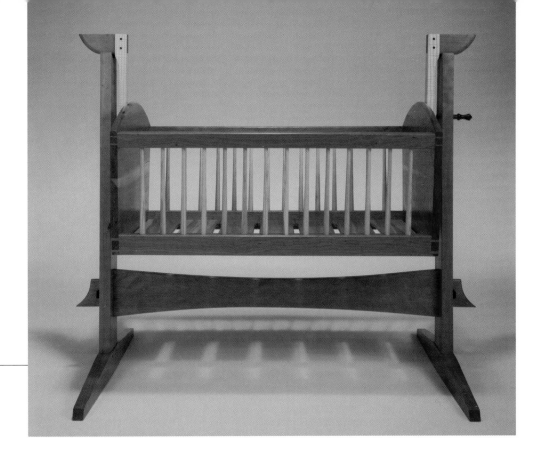

ROBBI STAPLES
Acushnet, Mass.

"Molly's Cradle"
Cherry, curly ash, bird's-eye
maple, walnut
43 in. x 24 in. x 37 in.
Photo by John Havens Thornton

RICK WISNIEWSKI
Neenah, Wis.

Twin-size canopy bed
Quartersawn sapele,
crotch mahogany
80 in. x 42 in. x 76 in.
Photo by Image Studios Inc.

JOHN W. GOFF
San Diego, Calif.

Neoclassical nightstands
Carelian birch, ebonized walnut,
Macassar ebony
30¼ in. x 17½ in. x 28¼ in.
Photo by Kevin Halle

TIMOTHY G. COZZENS
Chicago, Ill.

"Golden Cabbage Bed"
Cherry, beech veneer,
beech solid, pewter
90 in. x 72 in. x 48 in.

DAVID CRAMER
West Redding, Conn.

Bunny vanity
Cherry, satinwood,
basswood, pau amarillo
42 in. x 24½ in. x 73 in.
Photo by Laurie Klein

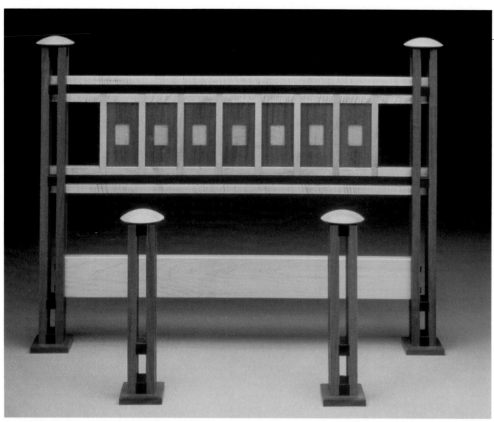

JONATHAN WRIGHT
Oberwil, Switzerland

Beds with solid or sandblasted
glass panels
Maple, mahogany, walnut, glass
(glass by Elena Sheppa)
84 in. x 63 in. x 47 in.
Photo by Dean Powell

DUNCAN W. GOWDY
La Mesa, Calif.

"Boxer Drawers"
Poplar, mahogany, white oak,
plywood, paint
20 in. x 24 in. x 75 in.
Photo by John Horner

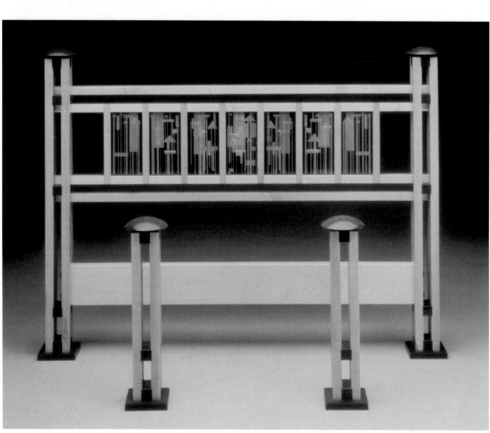

AARON GODFREY and
MATTHEW MOGER
Greensboro, N.C.

"Peanut"
Birch plywood, birch veneer
29 in. x 16 in. x 60 in.
Photo by Scott Croker

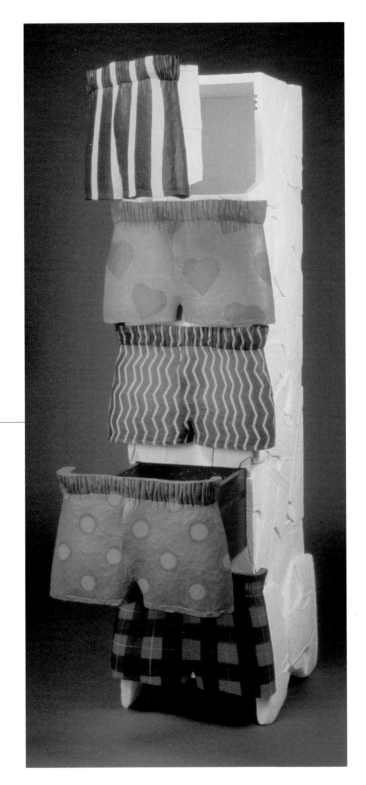

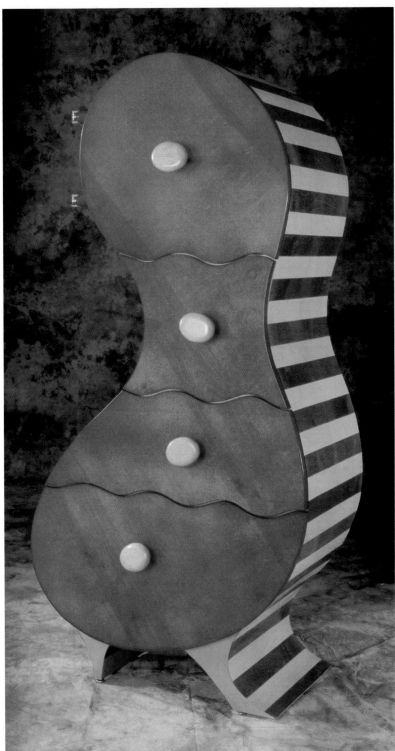

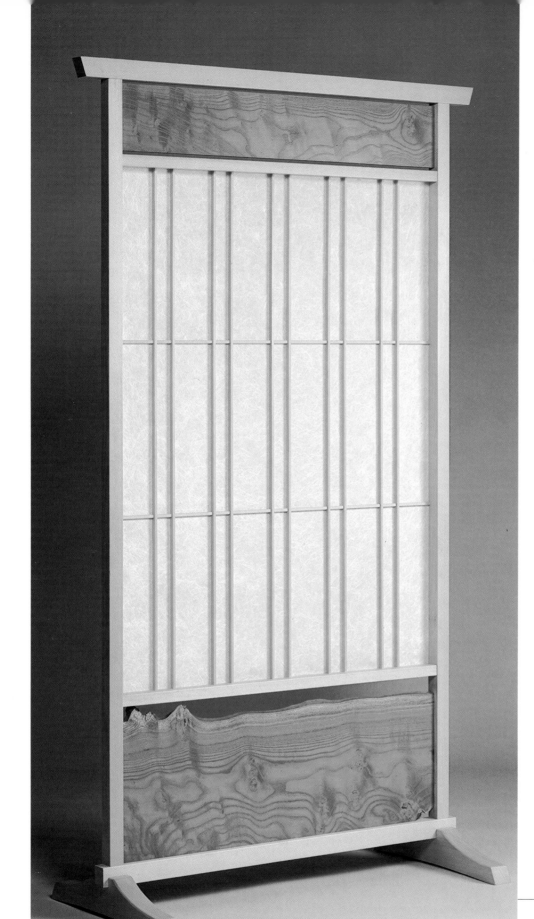

BOB REQUARTH
Paso Robles, Calif.

"Emily's Welcome"
Black walnut, red oak
60 in. x 30 in. x 45 in.
Photo by Scott Loy/Scott Loy
Photography

WILLEMSEN FOX
Newburyport, Mass.

Queen-size bed
Lacewood, ebonized ash
83 in. x 62 in. x 45 in.
Photo by Bill Truslow

MICHAEL CARROLL
Fort Bragg, Calif.

"Light and Shadows"
Port Orford cedar, mulberry,
mulberry paper
38 in. x 16 in. x 61 in.
Photo by Seth Janofsky

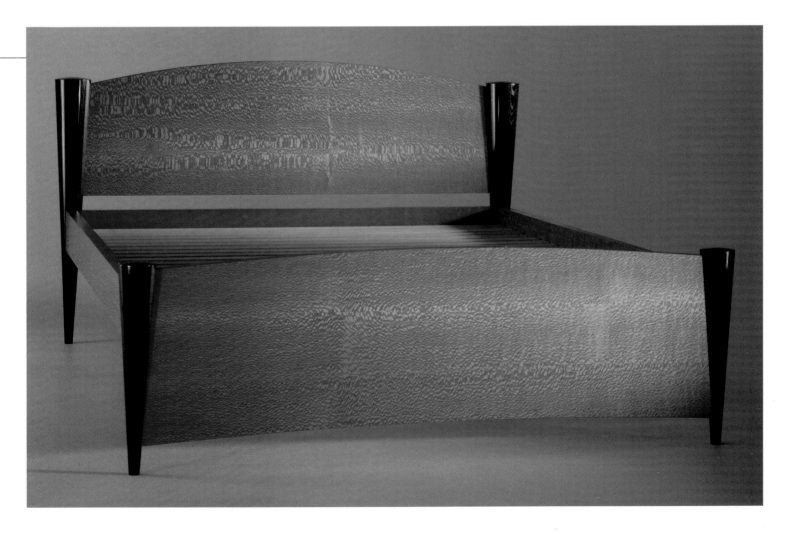

MAURICE E. and URSEL HOWLAND
Crawfordville, Fla.

Built-in closet
Black cherry, stained glass
82½ in. x 25½ in. x 95½ in.
Photo by Ursel and Maurice E. Howland

DAVID J. MARKS
Santa Rosa, Calif.

Inlaid bar
Bubinga, wenge, yellow
satinwood, ebony, purpleheart,
quilted mahogany, ziricote
26 ft. x 24 in. x 42 in.
Photo by Don Russel

WALTER O. JAEGER /
JAEGER & ERNST, INC.
Barboursville, Va.

"Camp"
Heart pine
48 in. x 16 in. x 96 in.
Photo by Philip Beaurline

MICHAEL STERLING
Chico, Calif.

Queen-size sleigh bed
Claro walnut solid, claro walnut
veneer, alder core
92½ in. x 73½ in. x 62 in.
Photo by Michael Agliolo

ROBERT J. SMITH
Grass Valley, Calif.

"Serafina's Cradle"
Purpleheart, cherry, maple
39 in. x 20 in. x 39 in.
Photo by Frank Pedrick

MICHAEL HUMPHRIES
Warwick, Mass.

"Arlene's Bed"
Hard and soft curly maple,
hard maple
86 in. x 68 in. x 40 in.
Photo by Donald H. Pugh

LARRY HAAS
Portsmouth, N.H.

Dresser
Cherry, glass, cloth
37½ in. x 23½ in. x 44 in.
Photo by Karosis Photographic

STEVEN M. WHITE
Berkeley, Calif.

Low dresser
Cherry, spalted maple
40 in. x 21 in. x 37 in.
Photo by Steven M. White

BRENT McGREGOR
Sisters, Ore.

Queen-size bed
Juniper
80 in. x 60 in. x 72 in.
Photo by Gary Alvis

MARC A. ADAMS
Franklin, Ind.

"Snow White Cradle"
Walnut, various veneers
for marquetry
36 in. x 24 in. x 32 in.
Photo by Marc A. Adams

sculpture
& carvings

FRED COGELOW
Willmar, Minn.

"Silent Soliloquy"
Basswood, butternut,
black walnut, birch
62 in. x 60 in. x 18-in. dia.
Photo by Bob Mischka

HAYWOOD NICHOLS
Savannah, Ga.

"Great Blue Heron"
Maple burl, black lacquer
15 in. x 15 in. x 68 in.
Photo by Joseph Byrd

JOHN T. SHARP
Kent, Ohio

"Still Life with Mallard & Apples"
Black walnut
36 in. x 24 in. x 25 in.
Photo by Gary Miller

MICHAEL J. BROLLY
Hamburg, Pa.

"Our Mother Hangs in the
Balance"
Mahogany, walnut, holly,
mixed veneers
22 in. x 14 in. x 18 in.
Photo by David Haas

BOB KOPEC
Longwood, Fla.

"Sanctuary"
Oak, lacquer, environ
21 in. x 7 in. x 6 in.
Photo by Bob Kopec

ROBERT LONGHURST
Chestertown, N.Y.

"Arabesque XXIX"
Bubinga
10½ in. x 9½ in. x 12 in.
Photo by Robert Longhurst

PETER GREEN
(Assembly and fabrication assisted by ANDY BORNUM, ANGELO IAFRATE and JOEL PENSLEY)
Westport, Conn.

"Trojan Birdhouse"
Maple, ash, cherry, brass, copper
38 in. x 12 in. x 32 in.
Photo by Peter Green

DENNIS ELLIOTT
Sherman, Conn.

Wall sculpture
Bigleaf maple burl, African blackwood, avonite, metal
40½ in. x 2½ in. x 33½ in.
Photo by Iona and Dennis Elliott

CHRISTIAN BURCHARD
Ashland, Ore.

"Chalice #14"
Madrone, mahogany
6 in. x 5 in. x 15 in.
Photo by Robert Jaffe

STEVE LOAR
(In collaboration with
ROBYN HORN)
Warsaw, N.Y.

"Pierced Geode/Early Spring"
Maple burl, purpleheart,
ink, paint
9 in. x 12-in. dia.
Photo by Bill DuBois

MICHAEL J. BROLLY
Hamburg, Pa.

"Maquette for Interplanetary
Harley Dude"
Mahogany, maple, ebony, cherry
20 in. x 22 in. x 10 in.
Photo by David Haas

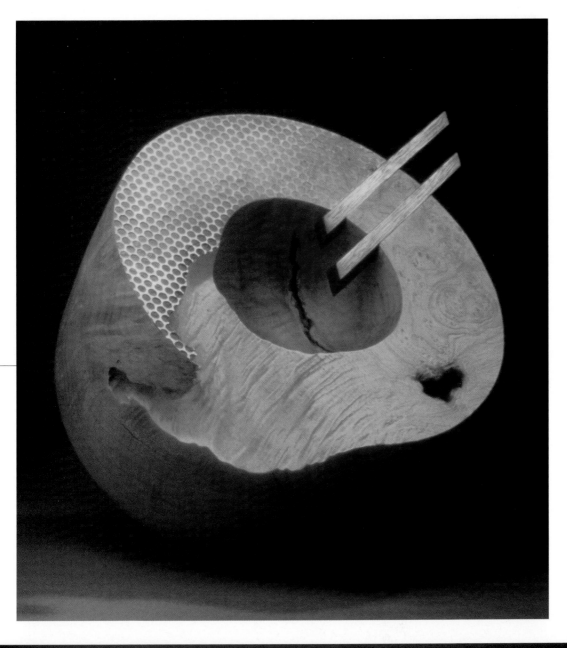

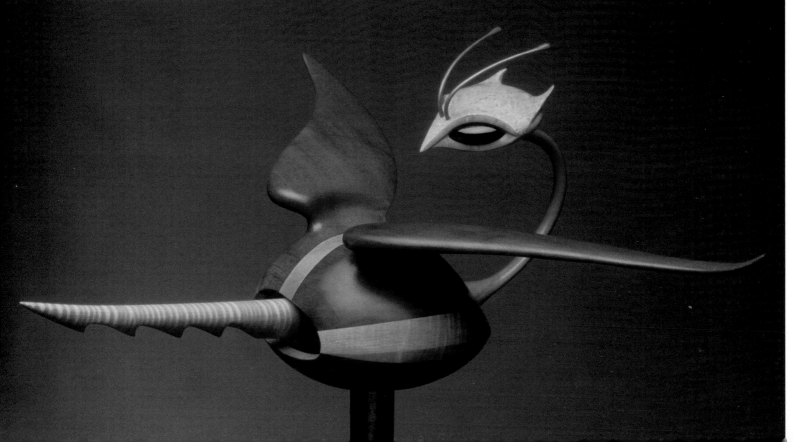

LARRY SIVELL
Maple Ridge, B.C., Canada

35mm motion picture camera
Cocobolo, curly maple,
padauk, bloodwood, cherry,
ebony, brass, glass
14½ in. x 6 in. x 9 in.
Photo by Ian Rushant

JESUS DOMINGUEZ
La Mesa, Calif.

"Josephine without Bananas"
Cocobolo, lignum vitae
78 in. x 14-in. dia.
Photo by Will Gullette

RODGER A. KAUFMAN
Ashland, Ohio

"Ark of the Covenant"
Maple
72 in. x 36 in. x 50 in.
Photo by Barry Finlay

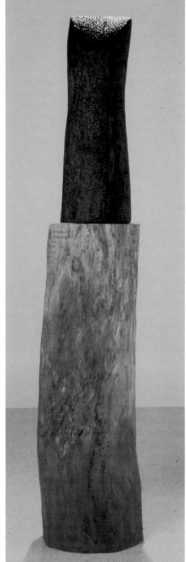

CHARLES ALLMOND
Wilmington, Del.

"Curlew"
Yew, walnut, maple, teak
15 in. x 4 in. x 17 in.
Photo by Eric R. Crossan

SHANE SHANE / SHANE 2
Belen, N.Mex.

"Feeding the Beast"
Purpleheart, pink ivory,
tulipwood, walnut
7 in. x 28 in. x 25 in.
Photo by Goffe Photographics

ROBERT E. FOJUT
Greendale, Wis.

"The Good Old Ordinary"
Basswood, cherry,
crank-driven bike
12 in. x 6 in. x 20 in.
Photo by Jim Wend

GEORGE RUTLEDGE
Petersburg, N.Y.

Rocking llama
White pine, cherry
44 in. x 13 in. x 35 in.
Photo by Herb Carter, Jr.

ROBERT LONGHURST
Chestertown, N.Y.

"Loop IL"
Bubinga
8 in. x 8 in. x 30 in.
Photo by Robert Longhurst

LEONARD H. FELDBERG
Chestnut Ridge, N.Y.

White wolves
Basswood, tupelo, mahogany
14 in. x 9 in. x 9 in.
Photo by Leonard H. Feldberg

GEORGE WORTHINGTON and
DENISE NIELSEN
Saugerties, N.Y.

Wooden hat
Cherry, walnut, padauk,
holly, poplar
15 in. x 16 in. x 10 in.
Photo by George Worthington

turnings

BARRY T. MACDONALD
Grosse Pointe, Mich.

Decanter
Bleached maple burl, bloodwood
15 in. x 8-in. dia.
Photo by Barry T. Macdonald

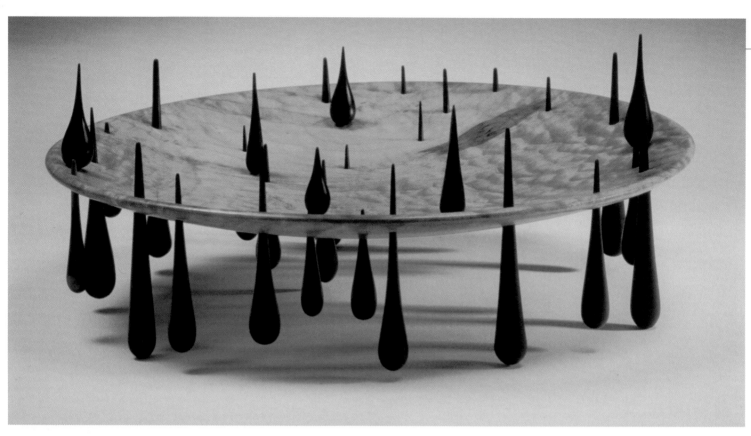

JOHN ECUYER
Whangarei, New Zealand

Solar temple offering bowl
Australian grass tree,
patinated copper
27½ in. x 13¾-in. dia.
Photos by John Ecuyer

WAYNE CAMERON
Saskatoon, Sask., Canada

"Acid Rain"
Quilted maple, African
blackwood
5⅞ in. x 13¾- in. dia.
Photo by Grant Kernan

JON SAUER
Daly City, Calif.

Mini-vase on pedestal
Blackwood, pink ivory,
cocobolo, zac nut
6¼ in. x 2½-in. dia.
Photo by Richard Sargent

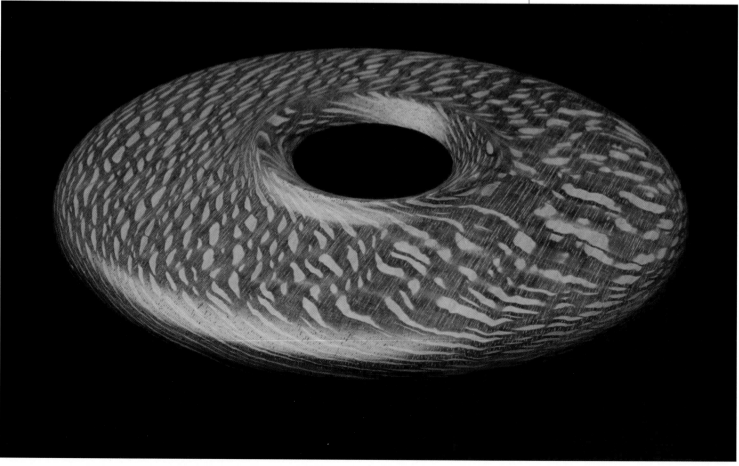

BERT AALBERS /
MEUBELMAKERJ KOPSHOUT
MB Numegen, The Netherlands

Bowl
Steamed beach, European maple,
copper
10⅝-in. dia.
Photos by Bert Aalbers/
Meubelmakerj Kopshout

BOB WOMACK
Cortez, Colo.

"Tribute to the Giants"
Redwood lace
13 in. x 8 in. x 17 in.
Photo by Pat Pollard

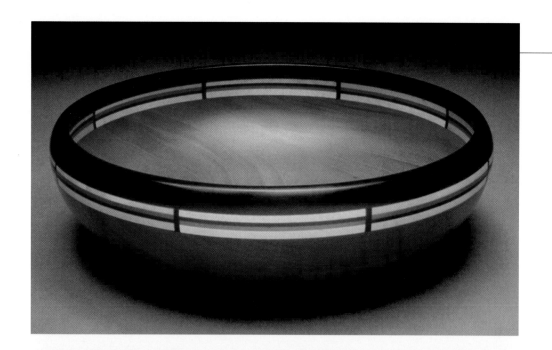

BETH IRELAND
Somerville, Mass.

Bowl
Mahogany, maple, ebony,
dyed veneer
2¾ in. x 12-in. dia.
Photo by John Horwor

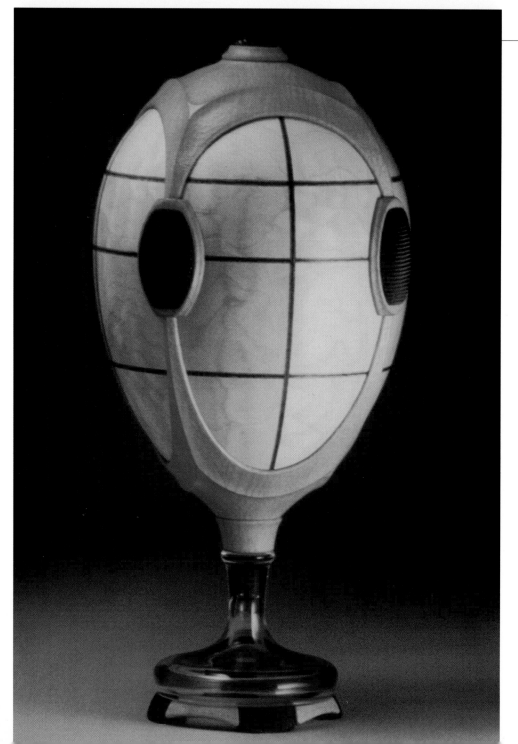

JIM HUME
Sedro Woolley, Wash.

Nested egg
Eastern maple, bleached quilted
maple, blue veneer, blue dyed
holly, acrylic
12⁹⁄₁₆ in. x 6⅜-in. dia.
Photo by Jim Hume

MARK SALWASSER
Arlington, Mass.

"The Bird Feeder"
Cherry
6 in. x 17-in. dia.
Photo by Mark Salwasser

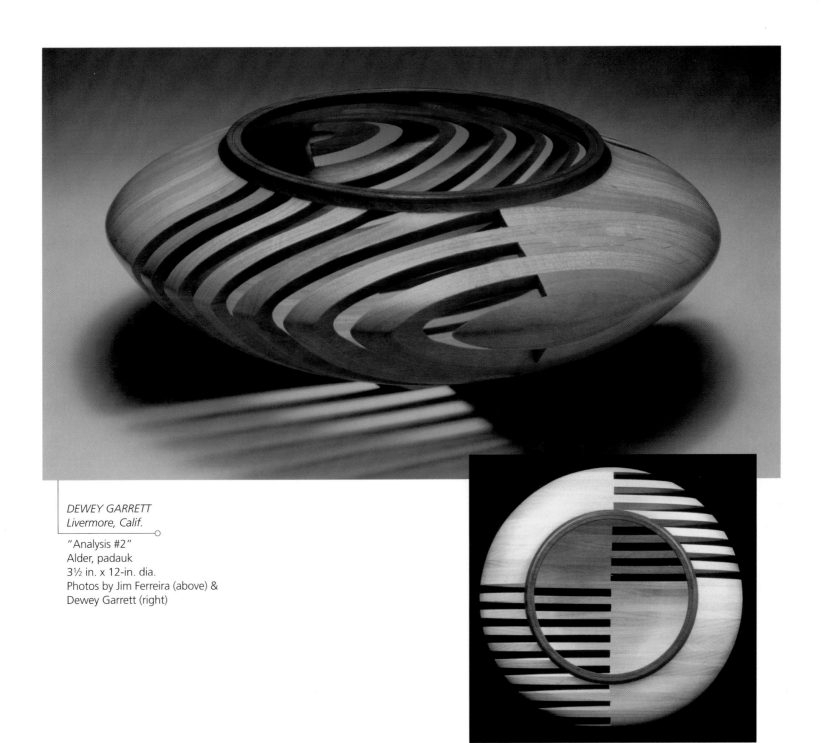

DEWEY GARRETT
Livermore, Calif.

"Analysis #2"
Alder, padauk
3½ in. x 12-in. dia.
Photos by Jim Ferreira (above) &
Dewey Garrett (right)

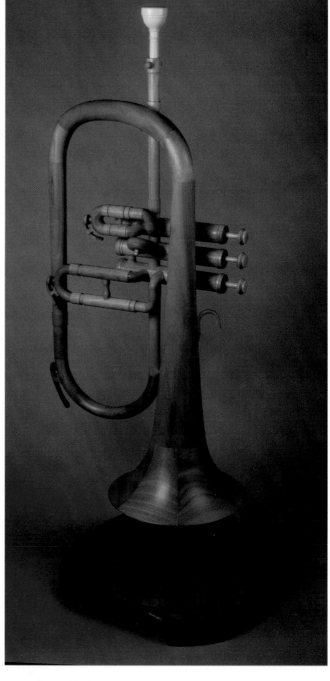

MICHAEL KORHUN
Troy, N.Y.

Vase
Paulownia, beads
12 in. x 10-in. dia.
Photo by Michael Korhun

ERIC L. MOREHOUSE
Waynesville, Mo.

Flügelhorn
Maple, holly, walnut, tagua nut,
mahogany
20¼ in. x 6 in. x 10 in.
Photo by Edward Chezick

ERIC L. MOREHOUSE
Waynesville, Mo.

Enclosed form
Spalted pine
5½ in. x 10-in. dia.
Photo by Edward Chezick

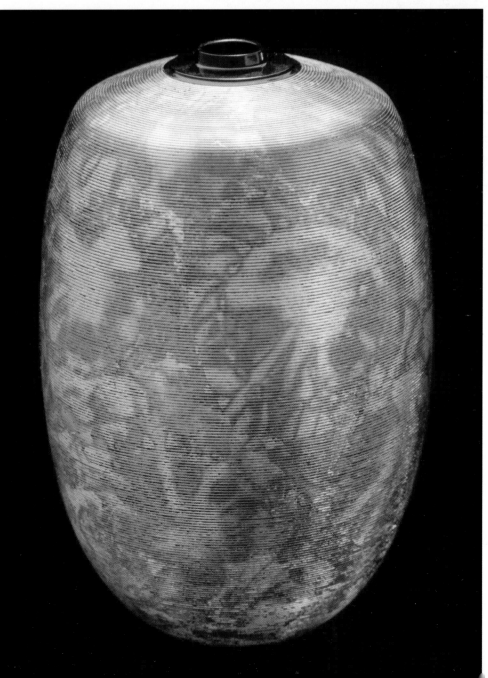

J. PAUL FENNELL
Scottsdale, Ariz.

"Metallica Green"
Citrus, variegated metal leaf,
black lacquer
8½ in. x 5½-in. dia.
Photo by Abrams Photographics

GEORGE RADESCHI
Doylestown, Pa.

"#87 Decorative Vessel"
Purpleheart, maple
27 in. x 29-in. dia.
Photo by Stephen Barth

BETH IRELAND
Somerville, Mass.

Bowl
Quilted maple
3½ in. x 11-in. dia.
Photo by Tom Nola

GARY JOHNSON
Bridgeton, Mo.

Reversible hollow form
Ziricote, birch
7 in. x 7-in. dia.
Photos by Eric Johnson

RAY ALLEN
Yuma, Ariz.

Southwest design bowl
Mesquite, maple, purpleheart,
satinwood, ebony, pecan,
rosewood
26 in. x 30-in. dia.
Photo by Ray Allen

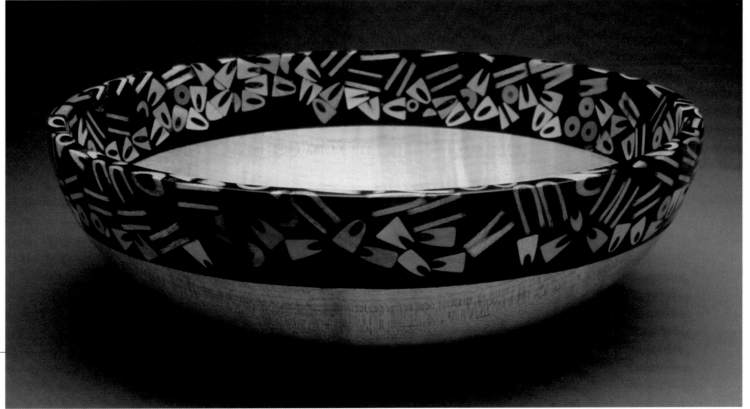

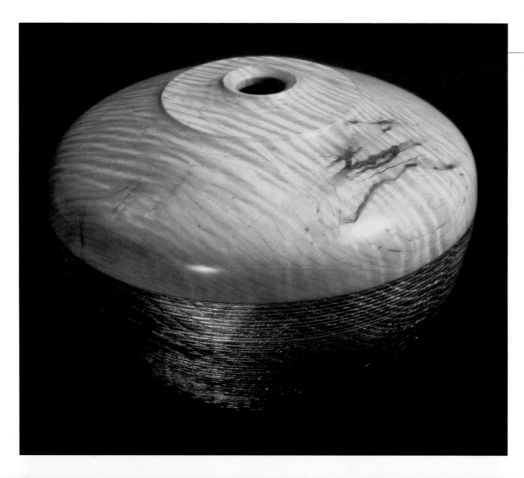

BRAHM FRIEDLANDER
Chatsworth, Ont., Canada

"Maple and Leaf"
Curly soft maple, red oak,
variegated copper leaf
16 in. x 12-in. dia.
Photo by Kris Rosar

CHRISTIAN BURCHARD
Ashland, Ore.

"Stepping Lightly/
Old Earth Series"
Mahogany, black paint
7-in. dia.
Photos by Robert Jaffe

ANDREW POTOCNIK
Macleod, West Vic., Australia

Bowl
Huon pine, stainless steel
4¼ in. x 13¼-in. dia.
Photo by Neil Thompson

BOB KOPEC
Longwood, Fla.

"Xylopot 520"
Black palm, wenge
1½ in. x 5-in. dia.
Photo by Bob Kopec

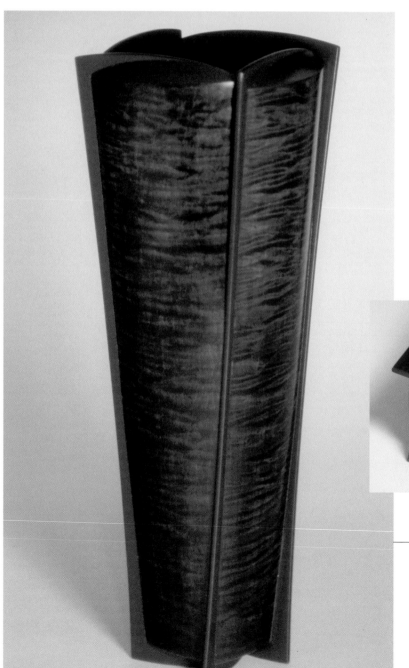

WAYNE RAAB
Canton, N.C.

"Blue Vase With a Twist"
Curly maple, soft maple, blue dye
17 in. x 5-in. dia.
Photos by Wayne Raab

GARY HINRICH
San Jose, Calif.

Tall vase
Purpleheart, black locust, black
walnut, cherry, holly, ficus, maple
39 in. x 17-in. dia.
Photo by Dynamic Focus
Photography

DEWEY GARRETT
Livermore, Calif.

"Ares"
Western maple burl
11½ in. x 6½-in. dia.
Photo by Jim Ferreira

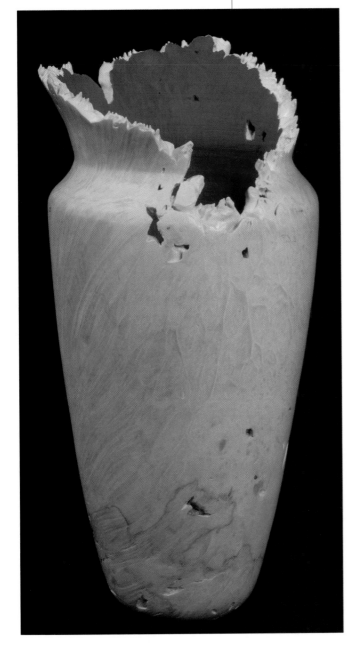

DENNIS ELLIOTT
Sherman, Conn.

Turned and carved vase
Bigleaf maple burl
14½ in. x 9½-in. dia.
Photo by Iona and Dennis Elliott

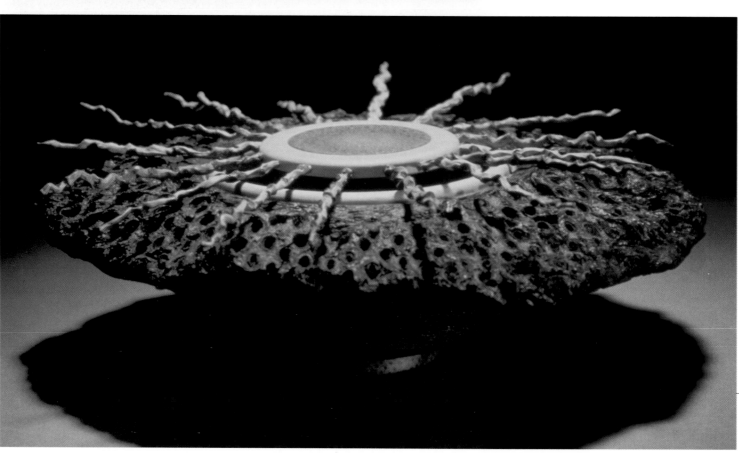

RON FLEMING
Tulsa, Okla.

"Madusa"
Cocobolo
13 in. x 7-in. dia.
Photo by Ron Fleming

GEOFFREY WILKES
Gerrardstown, W.Va.

"Black Textured Pot/
Ghost Vessel Series"
Ebonized cherry
3½ in. x 4-in. dia.
Photo by Geoffrey Wilkes

ANDREW POTOCNIK
Macleod, West Vic., Australia

Lidded container
Xanthorrea, huon pine
2⅛ in. x 6-in. dia.
Photo by Neil Thompson

PETER GREEN /
RENAISSANCE STUDIO
Westport, Conn.

Bowl with iridized and sand-
carved glass
Ash, glass inlay
4½ in. x 21-in. dia.
Photo by Peter Lukeris

GEOFFREY WILKES
Gerrardstown, W.Va.

"Pink Blush/Ghost Vessel Series"
Bleached box elder
6 in. x 5½-in. dia.
Photo by Geoffrey Wilkes

JON SAUER
Daly City, Calif.

Star boxes
Blackwood, kingwood,
tagua, pink ivory
3-4 in. x 2-4-in. dia.
Photo by Richard Sargent

MARK ALLEN BLAUSTEIN
Pittsburgh, Pa.

"The Tempest"
Maple, padauk, silver, copper,
Nugold, abalone, Corian
4 in. x 3½-in. dia.
Photos by Mark Allen Blaustein

accessories & musical instruments

PAULA GARBARINO
Somerville, Mass.

Classical guitar
Rosewood, cedar, mahogany,
ebony, bloodwood, cocobolo,
pernambuco
14½ in. x 4 in. x 39¼ in.
Photo by Meg Landsman

STEVEN WOODY PISTRICH
Hatfield, Mass.

Corner shelf
Walnut, curly soft maple
31 in. x 22 in. x 60 in.
Photo by David Keith

MALCOLM VAUGHAN
Bideford, Devon, England

Music stand
American walnut, maple,
rosewood peg
18 in. x 43 in. to 58 in.
Photo by Clive Boursnell

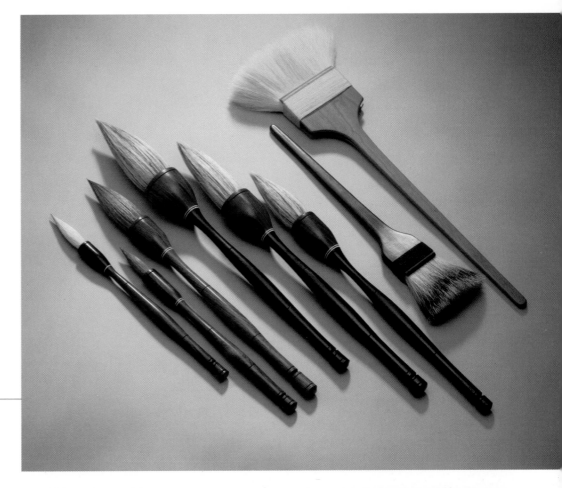

JOHN LEITCH
Santa Fe, N.Mex.

Oriental-style artist brushes
Cherry, cocobolo, ebony,
rosewood
8 in. to 14 in.
Photo by Michael Tincher

WILLIAM J. BURKE
Flagstaff, Ariz.

Mandolin
Maple, spruce, ebony
13 in. x 29 in.
Photos by William J. Burke

STEVEN ANDERSEN
Seattle, Wash.

"Oval Hole Arched-Top Guitar"
Engelmann spruce, bigleaf
maple, ebony
44 in. x 17 in.
Photo by Stacey Schofield

NIALL F. BARRETT
Narrowsburg, N.Y.

Table lamp
Bird's-eye maple, cedar, birch,
purpleheart, rosewood, fiberglass
26 in. x 8-in. dia.
Photo by Chris Holden

MICHAEL O'MAHONY
Bardwell Park, NSW, Australia

Five-string electronic fiddle
Australian red cedar, ebony,
European boxwood
8¼ in. x 23¼ in.
Photo by Terry Philpott

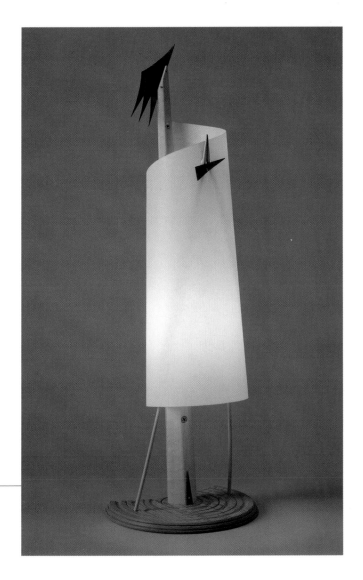

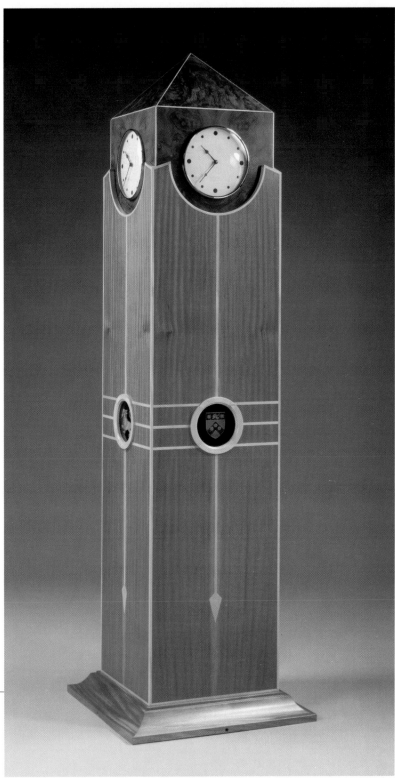

DALE BROHOLM
Wellesley, Mass.

Four-sided tall case clock
Mahogany, pau amarillo,
imbuia burl, ebony, glass
(glass by Elena Sheppa)
28 in. x 28 in. x 96 in.
Photo by Dean Powell

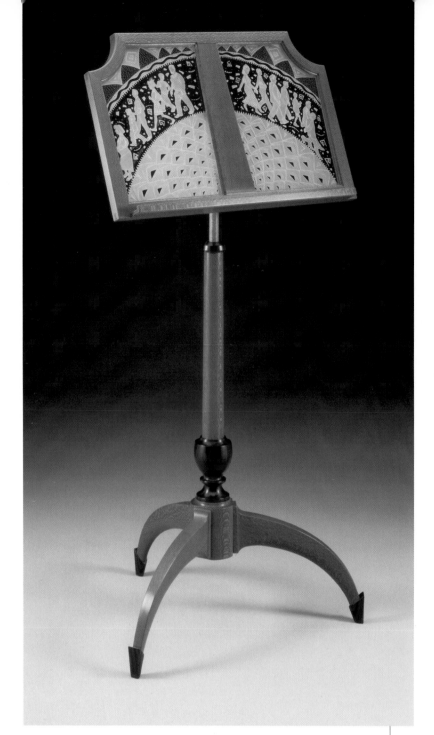

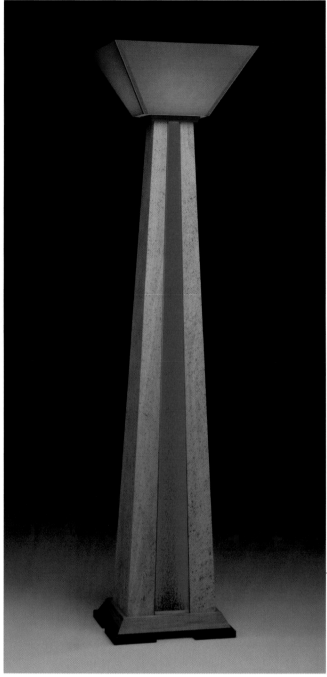

DALE BROHOLM
Wellesley, Mass.

Music stand
Oak, ebony, glass
(glass by Elena Sheppa)
36 to 46 in. x 26-in. dia.
Photo by Dean Powell

KEITH CORNELL
Cambridge, Mass.

Chip-carved bellows
Cherry, leather
20 in. x 9¼ in.
Photo by Lance Patterson

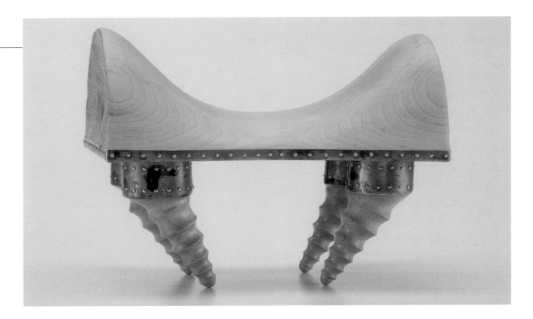

CHRISTOPHER SHEA
Smithville, Tenn.

Headrest
Maple, copper
12 in. x 7 in. x 8½ in.
Photo by John Lucas

MARK DEL GUIDICE
Norwood, Mass.

"Un Portrait Bleu En Torchére"
Peppered pecan, beefwood,
mahogany, canvas phenolic,
halogen, neon, black ground
glass
18 in. x 16 in. x 72 in.
Photo by Dean Powell

LEO KNAPP
Los Angeles, Calif.

Fretless bass guitar
Koa, Macassar ebony,
wenge, holly, graphite
13 in. x 3 in. x 45 in.
Photos by Alan Shaffer

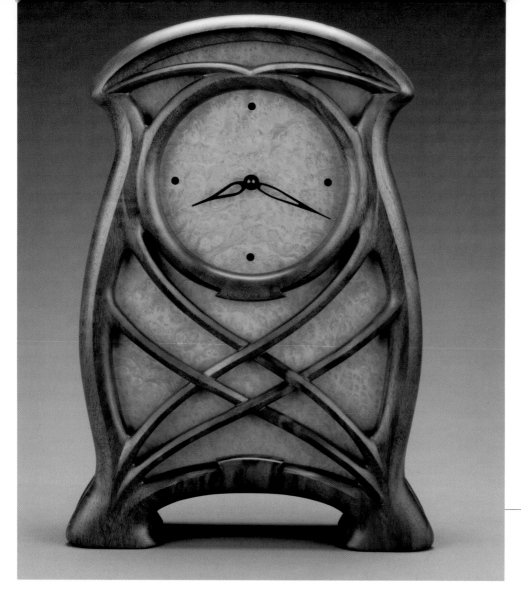

ROCHELLE CAMPBELL
Athens, Ga.

Music stand
Curly maple, padauk, mahogany
14 in. x 14 in. x 60 in.
Photo by Rochelle Campbell

LARRY ROHAN
Clinton, Wash.

Art Nouveau clock
Western walnut, Pacific
madrone burl
11 in. x 5 in. x 18 in.
Photo by Robert Vinnedge

RANDY MORRIS
Point Arena, Calif.

"The Dancer"
Wenge, purpleheart, cocobolo,
Honduran mahogany
12 in. x 17 in.
Photo by PJ McKay

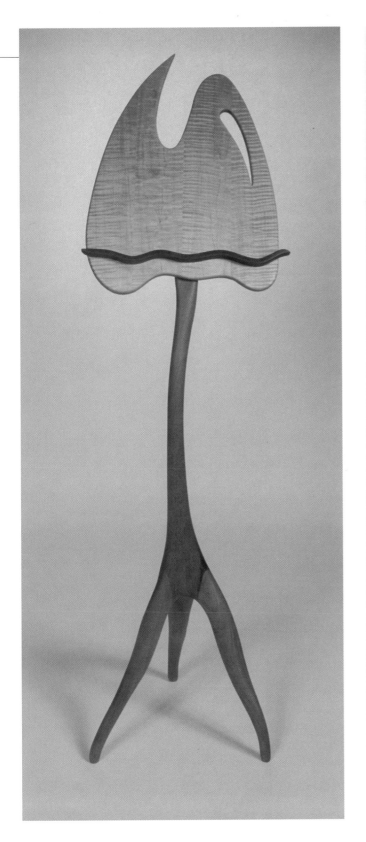

DOUGLAS FINKEL
Richmond, Va.

Music stand
Ebonized maple, padauk
22 in. x 8 in. x 48 in.
Photo by Mark Sfirri

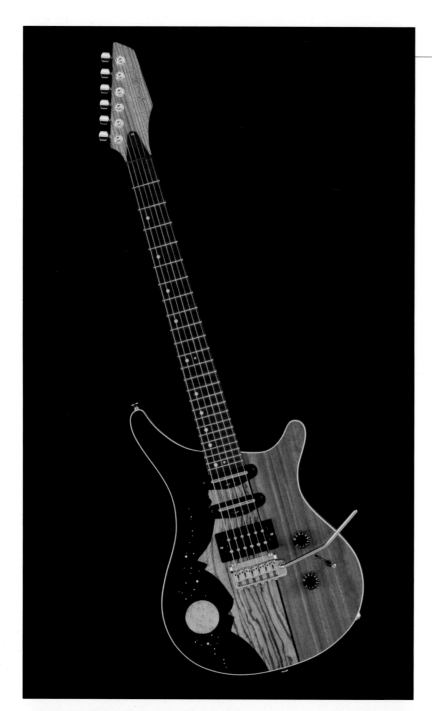

KEVIN GRAY
Dallas, Tex.

Custom electric guitar
Mahogany, ebony, zebra,
padauk, bird's-eye maple
12¼ in. x 1⅞ in. x 39 in.
Photo by David Hayes

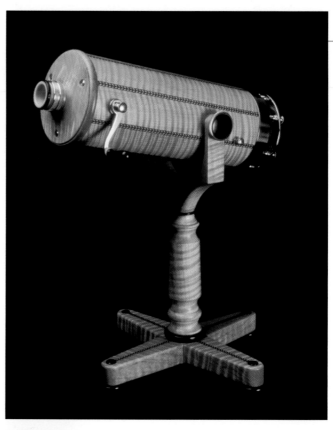

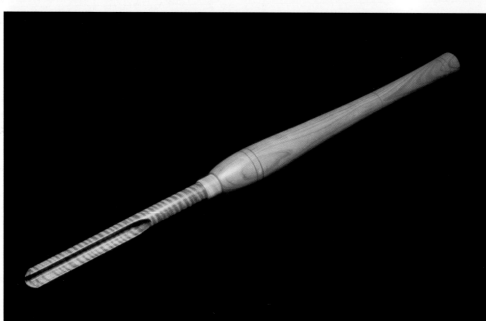

MARK SALWASSER
Arlington, Mass.

Wooden bowl gouge
Butternut, acrylic-impregnated
colored wood
26 in. x 1⅞-in. dia.
Photo by Tom Higgins

STEPHEN BRINK
St. Paul, Minn.

Table lamp
Quartersawn white oak,
stained glass
17 in. x 17 in. x 20 in.
Photo by Stephen Brink

J.R. BEALL
Newark, Ohio

"Nonpareil Kaleidoscope 2"
Fiddleback maple, ebony,
diamondwood
12¼ in. x 16¾ in. x 4¼-in. dia.
Photo by Judith Beall

STEVEN J. GRAY
Bozeman, Mont.

Tea set and grass schean
Walnut, ebony, maple burl
10 in. x 18 in. x 13 in.
Photo by Steven J. Gray

DENNIS THEISEN
Wyoming, Mich.

Electric candelabra
Black walnut, cherry, curly maple
8 in. x 4 in. x 20 in.
Photo by Dennis Theisen

GIDEON HUGHES
Portland, Ore.

"Shy Boy" self-portrait
Alder, birch plywood
16 in. x 16 in. x 76 in.
Photo by Maureen Kealy

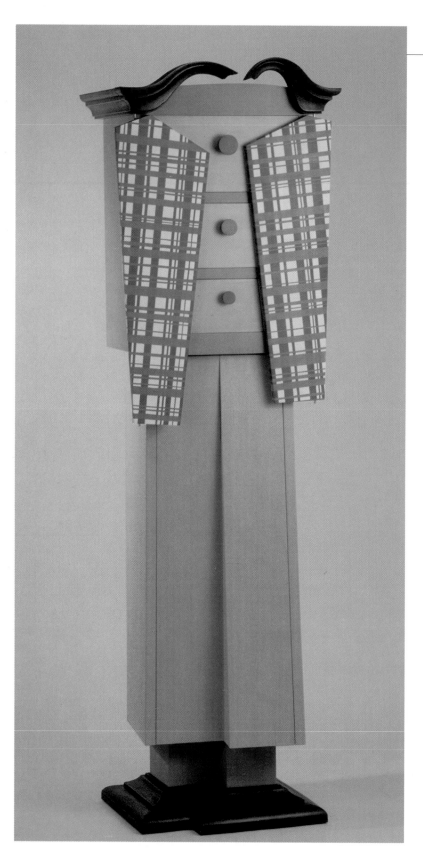

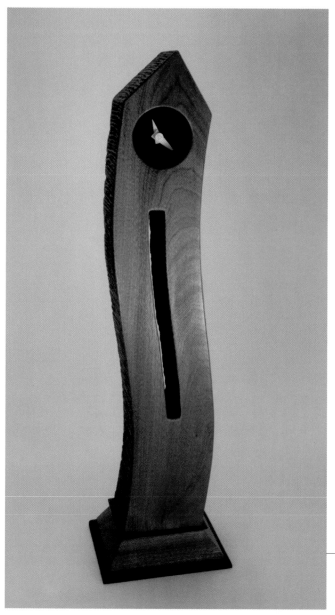

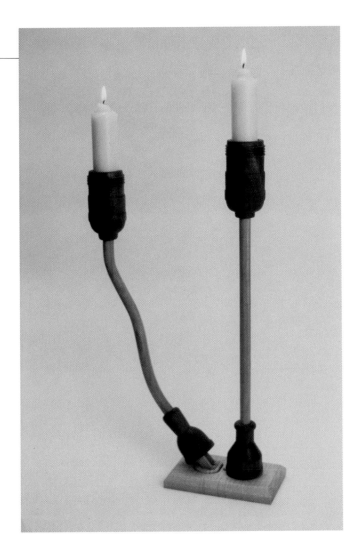

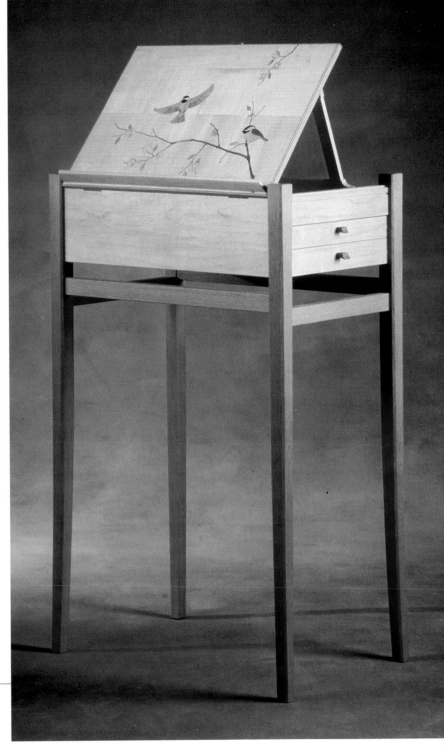

CRAIG VANDALL STEVENS
Sunbury, Ohio

"A Stand for Music"
Norway maple, white oak, yacca
24 in. x 15 in. x 49 in.
Photo by Stephen Webster

DENNIS THEISEN
Wyoming, Mich.

"When Bruno Met Garry..."
Honduran mahogany
8 in. x 8 in. x 33 in.
Photo by Dennis Theisen

ROBERT GIRDIS
Seattle, Wash.

Guitar
Myrtlewood, ebony, spruce
16 in. x 5 in. x 40 in.
Photos by John Sterling Ruth

JOHN L. SKAU
Archdale, N.C.

"X O X O X - Green"
Birch, maple
47¾ in. x 21-in. dia.
Photo by John L. Skau

NORM SARTORIUS
Parkersburg, W.Va.

Spoons
Amboyna burl
10 in. x 3 in. x 4 in.
Pink ivory
9½ in. x 3½ in. x 2 in.
Curly pink ivory
6½ in. x 1¼ in. x 1 in.
Photos by Jim Osborn

CRAIG R. PIERPONT
Edmonton, Ky.

36-string French-style harp
Cherry, Sitka spruce
30 in. x 14 in. x 52 in.
Photo by Craig R. Pierpont

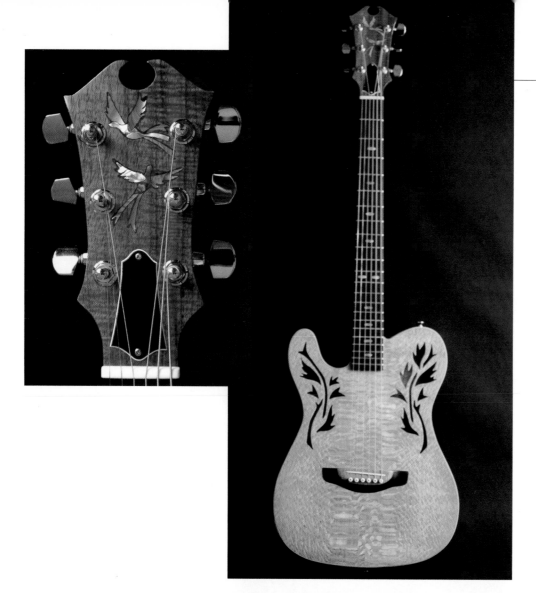

EDISON MUA
San Francisco, Calif.

Acoustic/electric left-handed
guitar
Lacewood, ebony, mahogany,
walnut, koa, abalone shell inlay
12¾ in. x 2 in. x 39 in.
Photos by Edison Mua

CLIVE TITMUSS
Surrey, B.C., Canada

17th-century French-style guitar
Rosewood, yew, recycled ivory,
ebony, parchment
9 in. x 4 in. x 37 in.
Photo by Kim Stallknecht

JEFF HUNT
San Francisco, Calif.

Table lamp
Cherry, Ebon-X,
cherry bark paper
13 in. x 13 in. x 21½ in.
Photo by George Post

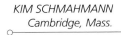

KIM SCHMAHMANN
Cambridge, Mass.

Grandparent clock
Mahogany
18 in. x 10 in. x 90 in.
Photo by Lance Patterson

index

Publisher: *Jim Chiavelli*
Acquisitions Editor: *Rick Peters*
Publishing Coordinator: *Joanne Renna*

Designer/Layout Artist: *Christopher Casey*
Copy/Production Editor: *Diane Sinitsky*

Typeface: *Frutiger*
Paper: *Somerset Gloss, 80 lb.*
Printer: *R. R. Donnelley, Willard, Ohio*